THE HOPE OF
HEAVEN

Other Books by Sheila Walsh

It's Okay Not to Be Okay

It's Okay Not to Be Okay Study Guide

Praying Women

Praying Women Study Guide

Praying Girls Devotional

Holding On When You Want to Let Go

Holding On When You Want to Let Go Study Guide

The Gifts of Christmas

THE HOPE OF
HEAVEN

HOW THE PROMISE OF ETERNITY
CHANGES EVERYTHING

SHEILA WALSH

BakerBooks

a division of Baker Publishing Group
Grand Rapids, Michigan

© 2024 by Sheila Walsh

Published by Baker Books
a division of Baker Publishing Group
Grand Rapids, Michigan
BakerBooks.com

Printed in the United States of America

Library of Congress Cataloging-in-Publication Data
Names: Walsh, Sheila, 1956– author.
Title: The hope of heaven : how the promise of eternity changes everything / Sheila Walsh.
Description: Grand Rapids, Michigan : Baker Books, a division of Baker Publishing Group, [2024] | Includes bibliographical references.
Identifiers: LCCN 2023054043 | ISBN 9781540900272 (cloth) | ISBN 9781493447077 (ebook)
Subjects: LCSH: Future life—Christianity.
Classification: LCC BT903 .W563 2024 | DDC 236/.2—dc23/eng/20240130
LC record available at https://lccn.loc.gov/2023054043

ISBN 978-1-5409-0484-3 (ITPE)

Jacket design by Laura Powell
Jacket artwork © Gold Linings by Sadie Wilson

The author is represented by Dupree Miller and Associates, a global literary agency, www.dupree miller.com

Baker Publishing Group publications use paper produced from sustainable forestry practices and post-consumer waste whenever possible.

24 25 26 27 28 29 30   7 6 5 4 3 2 1

This book is dedicated to all who have a
deep longing for more than this world offers.
What you are longing for is heaven.
This is our eternal hope.

CONTENTS

INTRODUCTION

CAN YOU HELP ME?

"I'm fed up with earth."

This very odd and unfamiliar feeling had been growing in my heart for months. An expanding internal list of all that is wrong in this world was weighing me down.

The evening news with its never-ending pictures of war decimating towns and villages. The haunted faces of children and older adults walking through the rubble of what was their lives, holding onto the little that was left.

Then came stories that are closer to home.

A friend facing a returning cancer diagnosis for the third time.

The onslaught of anxiety, depression, and loneliness.

Familiar and trusted faces walking away from their faith as if it was a childhood tale they had outgrown.

So much pain, so much despair, so much anger, so much loss.

I was carrying a sadness and weariness I'd never felt before. And yet, there was one more weight added that would ironically lead me to the most hope-filled place I've ever been. But it didn't start that way.

It started out as something very ordinary, very simple. I was cleaning out my bathroom cabinet drawers (cleaning makes me happy). I read a book once that said you should hold up everything you own and ask yourself if it makes you happy. If it does, keep it, if not, toss it. I'd already thrown out the bathroom scale, as it had never brought me any joy, so now I was onto round two. I began tossing out old cans of hairspray and mostly empty jars of face cream. At the bottom was a jar of my favorite cream. I opened the jar and saw that there was just a little cream remaining at the very bottom and around the edges. I'm Scottish, so not wanting to waste it, I scraped every bit out with my fingernail and spread it onto the palms of my hands. In that moment, I realized I should have tied my hair back first, as it was falling onto my face. So I bent my head over, then lifted it up and flipped my hair back in one simple, quick movement.

That was all it took. I heard a snap, and pain shot from my neck down my back. I couldn't move my head. I had no idea what to do next. I fell onto my knees and rested my forehead on the cold marble at the edge of the sink. How could a simple movement I've done a million times before cause so much pain? I was panic-stricken, scared to move in case I did more damage. I needed help, but my husband, Barry, was downstairs and my phone was on the bed. I tried calling his name, but the television was on, and I had no strength in my voice. Tears began to roll down my face as I prayed, "God, please help me. I don't know what to do."

I shuffled on my knees out of the bathroom and into the bedroom, each movement making me sick to my stomach. I grabbed my phone and texted Barry.

"Can you help me?!"

I heard Barry take the stairs two at a time, bounding in with our dog Maggie at his heels. "What's wrong?" he asked. "Are you okay?"

When he saw me kneeling beside the bed with tears rolling down my cheeks, his face lost all its color.

"Sheila, what happened?" he cried.

"I think I might have broken my neck," I whispered.

Neither of us knew what to do. He asked me if I could stand. I told him that I didn't know if I could, but if he helped me, I would try. He put his arm under mine and helped me to my feet. The room began to spin, and I was violently sick. We knew I needed to get to the emergency room as quickly as possible. Neither of us could remember where the closest emergency room was. (Isn't it funny that when you don't need something, you see it all the time until you do need it, and then all memory of where it was is gone.) Barry googled "closest ER" and saw that it was just five miles away. With his help, I was able to gradually get down the stairs and slowly lower myself into the passenger seat of the car. Every tiny bump in the road felt terrifying, causing me to cry out in pain. I was so afraid that I would do more damage and end up paralyzed. By the time we got to the hospital, I was gasping for air. I've never had a panic attack before, but from what others have told me, that's what it felt like. I felt out of control and afraid.

I was shaking so badly that I couldn't walk, so Barry found a wheelchair and wheeled me to the registration desk. The receptionist asked a few questions and began to take notes. Then she stopped typing, looked up from her screen, and turned to face me. "Stop taking such short breaths," she said. "You're making things worse."

I'm sure I turned beet red. I felt as if I was five years old and had just been reprimanded by the teacher for daydreaming in class. Being Scottish and a true Brit, I immediately apologized. (We are renowned for apologizing for everything, whether we've done something wrong or not. We assume it's the right thing to do. We think, "What would the queen have done?")

"Like this," she said, taking long, slow breaths. "Breathe with me, like this." I did and it became much easier to catch my breath. She called for a nurse who fixed a large hard plastic brace around my neck. Wheeling me into the waiting room, she told us, "We're very busy today. The average wait time is about four hours." My heart dropped.

The waiting room was noisy and crowded. I sat with my eyes closed. I had a childlike urge to call my mom, but she had been gone for several years. I wasn't used to feeling afraid. Barry hates going to the doctor. He thinks if he does, they'll find something wrong with him, but if he doesn't go, he'll be fine. That thought would never cross my mind. I always assume I'm fine and if there is something wrong, they'll fix it. This felt different, and it shook me.

I am a Christian. Not a "goes to church on Easter and Christmas" person who has a Bible somewhere in a drawer, but an "all-in, I believe that the Bible is true, God is my Father, Jesus is my closest friend, and the Holy Spirit is my comforter" Christian. So no matter what happens in my life, I believe that God has a purpose for it. I've gone through hard things before. I've had a large tumor removed. I've had an invasive back surgery and lots of other things I didn't see coming, as I'm sure you have too. So why did this feel so different? As I sat in the waiting room at the beginning of what would be a very long night, that was the question I turned over and over in my mind. It felt as if the weight of the world was crushing me.

Eventually, in the early evening, I was taken back to a cubicle where I was able to lie down. I was in a lot of pain, so Barry asked the nurse if I could have some pain medication. She said that she was sorry but that wouldn't be possible until I had a CT scan and an MRI. It took hours, but finally all the tests were done, and we waited for an answer. At about six o'clock in the morning, eighteen hours after the injury, a neurosurgeon came in looking as if he hadn't slept much either. He held up an image of my neck and silently studied it. I felt fear creeping in again. I didn't know what he was going to tell me.

Thankfully it was good news. The only damage I'd done was tear some ligaments in my neck, and although very painful, they would heal on their own. I was very grateful. But I still needed an answer to why I felt desperately burdened by so many things.

I needed an answer, and I found it. I should have known where to look. It's where I always find not only answers but peace and truth and love and hope. I don't know whether the Bible is significant in your life, but for me, when everything else in the world seems upside down, God's Word is right side up. Some think of the Bible as a crutch, but to me it's a love letter. It's a life-giving bridge from the brokenness of this world to the very heart of a good and faithful God.

> **When everything else in the world seems upside down, God's Word is right side up.**

So after this hospital scare, I began a deep dive. This is the first thing I read as I searched for answers. It changed my heart and, honestly, gave birth to this book.

> Keep your eyes on *Jesus*, who both began and finished this race we're in. Study how he did it. Because he never lost sight of where he was headed—that exhilarating finish in and with God—he could put up with anything along the way: Cross, shame, whatever. And now he's *there*, in the place of honor, right alongside God. (Heb. 12:2–3 MSG)

Those words stood out as if in neon lights: "He never lost sight of where he was headed." Because he never lost sight of where he was headed—that exhilarating finish in and with God—he could put up with anything along the way. Jesus came from heaven and was willing to endure the greatest human suffering ever to make it possible for you and me to join him there forever.

Heaven changes everything. So I began to dig deep. I wanted to remind myself of everything I already knew about heaven and find out all the things I'd missed. I want to tell you here, right up front, it's been life-changing. If we begin to grasp a picture of the hope that's waiting for us in heaven, it will impact every single day we have here on earth. I'll try and answer some of the questions you might have. But more than that, it's my prayer that God, through the person and power of the Holy Spirit, will light such a fire in your heart that nothing can extinguish it. We have a promise of an everlasting hope that changes everything.

> Since you have been raised to new life with Christ, set your sights on the realities of heaven, where Christ sits in the place of honor at God's right hand. Think about the things of heaven, not the things of earth. For you died to this life, and your real life is hidden with Christ in God. And when Christ, who is your life, is revealed to the whole world, you will share in all his glory. (Col. 3:1–4)

What would it take in your understanding of heaven to change how you live right now? What are the questions you would love answers to? Does disappointment with your life on earth impact what you think heaven will be like?

Being fed up with earth absolutely makes sense to me now. We were made for more. The yearning you and I feel at times, even on our best days, is because we were made for heaven and nothing else will do. So let's unpack all we can about our eternal hope. It will change everything.

1

IS HEAVEN REALLY REAL?

Don't let your hearts be troubled. Trust in God, and trust also in me. There is more than enough room in my Father's home. If this were not so, would I have told you that I am going to prepare a place for you? When everything is ready, I will come and get you, so that you will always be with me where I am.

John 14:1–3

Home.

For most of us that word suggests a place where we belong, where we are safe and loved, peaceful and welcomed. For me, it also means endless shelves of books, a comfy sofa to sink into, a soft blanket, and a basket of toys by the fire for our Yorkie, Maggie. I love to sit outside on our balcony with that first cup of coffee every morning while Maggie barks at passing cars. But the peace of those quiet mornings changed in the winter of 2021.

Our balcony overlooks a lane that separates the homes on our street from the ones a street over. The house that is directly behind us had been empty for almost three years. I wasn't sure who owned the house, so I tried to keep an eye on it, but it gradually fell deeper and deeper into disrepair. Then, one morning came a deafening noise. A bulldozer arrived to tear it all down. Our balcony became the resting place for layer upon layer of dust and dirt. Then came the rats. Yes, I said rats. Apparently they had been squatters since the previous owners moved out. One of the rats became a regular visitor to our yard. I called him Mr. Whiskers. He was the size of a small cat. Barry and our pest control guy came up with a plan to "relocate" our whiskered friends. As a lover of animals great and small, that's all I want to say about that.

Then came the port-a-john. I didn't know that one had arrived until I tried to back out of our garage one morning and almost knocked it over! I'm glad I didn't, as it had an occupant inside at the time. When he came out, I wasn't sure whether to wave or apologize so I did both. He waved back. As we still have towers of toilet tissue piled up in our garage from the *we're-in-a-worldwide-pandemic-so-buy-more-toilet-tissue* situation that never quite made sense to me, I wondered if I should offer some, but decided against it. Barry called the number on the side of the port-a-john, and they moved it further into the now-vacant lot. I scrubbed our balcony down, washed the windows, and got rid of the layers of dirt, and for two blissful weeks the only noise to disturb the morning quiet was Maggie barking at the occasional squirrel.

It was so peaceful. But that's not the end of this story.

Another crew arrived. This time it was a construction crew to begin the rebuild. I don't know where they got a radio that can play at a volume heard two zip codes over, but they had one. By early spring, our poor Maggie was so worn out from barking that she just lay on her back in her basket, resigned to an apparently meaningless life. It gets unbearably hot in Texas in the summer months, so I understood why the workers would want to start earlier in the day, but we were now gifted with a daily blasting of country songs at 7:00 a.m. We had a reality show we could watch right from our balcony in our very own home.

But all the chaos got me thinking. These were all just earthly annoyances, but what about the questions that had been growing in my heart for more than this present life can deliver? I wanted to find out what this ache was all about. I first started to think about home, about Scotland, and how much I miss my family. I thought about how many of the people I knew as a child are no longer with us. Amid all my nostalgic reminiscing, the answer came. It had been staring me in the face all along. What I was longing for was the ultimate promise, our ultimate future, our ultimate hope: heaven.

What comes to your mind when you think of heaven? Some think of us floating around on clouds playing a harp, others of being greeted at the pearly gates by long-lost pets. (We will address the important "Do dogs go to heaven?" question later in the book.) As a teenager, my idea of heaven was very vague. I couldn't imagine what we would do year after year. I had an idea that singing would be involved, but what would we sing and for how long, and wouldn't that get old after a couple of thousand years? I wondered about flying. That was an idea that was very appealing to me, but where would we be going, and would we know when we got there, and would we be able to find our way back to our designated spot? I was most concerned by the thought that if everyone who has ever followed Jesus would be in heaven too, how would I ever get a glimpse of him as the crowd would be so huge?

Our ideas of what heaven will be like are usually colored by our own families and where we grew up, whether our family was a family of faith, just popped into church occasionally, or never gave faith a second thought. I grew up in Scotland, a country where many people get sentimental about the idea of heaven only when someone they love dies. They'll raise a glass to them, assuming that heaven's pub opened up and welcomed them in. In 2022 the Scottish government carried out a survey asking people if they identified as Christians. Thirty-three percent said that they did, but only a quarter of those said that they believed that Jesus was a real person, the Son of God.[1]

So what does it even mean to be a Christian within those param-
eters? There seems to be more fuzzy, wishful thinking involved than
personal life-changing, relational faith. When it comes to heaven,
the apparent assumption is that whatever their relatives or friends
were doing on earth before they died, they would simply carry on
in heaven. But that's not what God's Word teaches us. The truth
about heaven is so much greater than this. It is life-changing. It's
what we were made for.

I believe that when we grasp a proper understanding of the reality
of heaven, it will change every single day we have here on earth. For
those of us who are in relationship with Christ, the reality of heaven
as our forever home should be even more real than the things we
see all around us every day. For many of us though, we're not quite
sure what that means or what it will look like. So it's my passionate
commitment in this book to share the only real truth about heaven:
what the Bible says.

Heaven is a real place.

Heaven is for real people.

Heaven is where we'll be with our real Savior forever.

Heaven is everywhere in the Bible, from Genesis to Revelation.
Did you know that there are at least six hundred references to the
word *heaven* in the Bible? Jesus talks about heaven around seventy
times just in Matthew's Gospel. But let me ask
you, how many sermons have you heard about
what heaven will be like, what we'll do, how
we'll live? I've not heard many. I've listened to
lots of sermons on the sacrifice Christ paid
to secure our place in heaven, but almost none about heaven and
what we'll do when we get there. So in this first chapter, I want us to
look together at the assurance that Christ gave to his closest friends
about the reality of heaven. On the night when he was about to be
betrayed, he knew that in their eyes, everything was going to seem
as if it had gone terribly wrong. He said to them,

"I am going to prepare a place for you."

Don't let your hearts be troubled. Trust in God, and trust also in me. There is more than enough room in my Father's home. If this were not so, would I have told you that I am going to prepare a place for you? When everything is ready, I will come and get you, so that you will always be with me where I am. (John 14:1–3)

Let's look at what Jesus said and why it was so life-changing.

1. "Don't let your hearts be troubled."

I can't think of a disease that affects each one of us more than a troubled, anxious heart. Every single one of us is going to face heartache, sometimes over and over again. There are so many things we didn't see coming:

loneliness
fear
bankruptcy
loss of a job
an unexpected diagnosis
a son or daughter lost in a world of drugs
divorce

The list could go on and on. So why, knowing everything that was going to happen to the disciples that night, knowing everything that you and I were going to have to face in our lives, would Jesus tell them, and us, not to be troubled? He didn't say that trouble doesn't exist. He didn't say that his death and resurrection were going to wipe out trouble. So why did he tell us not to be troubled?

If you read John 13, it becomes clear why Jesus said that to his friends that night. He had just done something that would have seemed outrageous to them.

So he got up from the table, took off his robe, wrapped a towel around his waist, and poured water into a basin. Then he began to wash the disciples' feet, drying them with the towel he had around him. (John 13:4–5)

It was not unusual to have your feet washed upon entering a Jewish home. Wearing open-toed sandals on dusty roads meant that it was normal for a dinner host to arrange for a servant to greet guests at the door and wash their feet. But to see Jesus, their leader, kneel before them was unheard of. Peter initially refused in very strong terms to have his feet washed by Jesus. The original Greek language translates, "You will never in all eternity wash my feet!" When Jesus responded that unless he allowed him to wash his feet, he would never belong to him, Peter said, "Then wash me all over!" Jesus told his passionate, if confused, friend that that was not necessary. Then he told each one of them that just as he had done, they should wash each other's feet. I remember we read this passage in our youth group when I was about sixteen. We took the text very literally, and for weeks we all had the cleanest feet in Scotland.

So that was the first thing that was different in this passage. But as the evening continued, it was clear to everyone in the room that Christ became deeply troubled. He told them that one of them was about to betray him. They were horrified and tried to work out among themselves who Jesus was talking about. John was sitting beside Jesus, so Peter motioned to him to ask who it was. Jesus dipped bread in a bowl and said it was the one he gave the bread to. In those days it was a sign of friendship or honor for someone to give bread to another. Christ offered it to Judas. Would he take it? I've often wondered if it was Judas's last chance to change his mind and heart. But we read that when Judas took the bread, Satan entered him. The rest of the disciples didn't seem to understand what was going on. But perhaps the most troubling statement of the night was when Jesus turned to Peter and said to him, "I tell you the truth, Peter—before the rooster crows tomorrow morning, you will deny three times that you even know me" (John 13:38).

By now, they were all deeply concerned. The rest of the disciples knew that Peter could be a bit loud and arrogant at times, but they would never have questioned his loyalty to Jesus. This was a shocking statement, so why would Jesus tell them not to be troubled in John 14:1? He knew that for them, and for you and me, things will happen that make us feel as if life is out of control, and in those moments, in those very moments, we will have to choose to hold on to the truth of Christ's promises. Then Jesus spoke again.

2. "Trust in God, and trust also in me."

This is such a powerful command. Think about it. Jesus knew that the next hours and days would make no sense to them; it would feel as if their world had fallen apart. He was saying to them, and to you and me, don't trust in what you see or what makes sense to you; trust in God your Father and trust in me. What a word for us in these crazy days. How many times have things in your life gone in directions that make no sense at all and it feels as if your life is out of control? Perhaps you are there right now. Jesus says trust in God and trust in him. This is not wishful thinking. This is a rock-solid invitation from Christ to intentionally choose to place our trust in him no matter what is going on around us.

Not only that, he's also saying that we can't trust in ourselves to be all that we wish we could be. Just like Peter, we will fail, we will fall. Have you been there? It's so easy when that happens to lose heart and give up hope, but Jesus is saying that we don't have to trust in ourselves, we can place our trust firmly in Christ.

I fall so far short of the standard that Christ set. He lived a selfless life. When he spoke out in anger, it was always about the right thing and it was never for his own benefit. It was always about those who muddied the picture of who God is to others. It was pure. But that's not always the case in our own lives. I see that so often in myself, even in the smallest things.

While I was writing this chapter, Barry asked me to stop for a while and help him with something. A simple request. Out of the blue, I got frustrated with him because I was busy writing. The irony is not lost on me. As I get older, I am more aware of the grace and mercy of God, but I'm also more aware of how very short I fall. When I feel this way, it reminds me of Peter. When Jesus told the disciples that he would only be with them a little while longer, Peter didn't understand. In his mind, if Jesus was leaving, he was going with him, even if he had to die with him. That's when he heard those words that would haunt him in the hours to come after the rooster crowed three times. But like Peter, when we do fail, Christ lays a path of grace for us to find our way back home.

> **But like Peter, when we do fail, Christ lays a path of grace for us to find our way back home.**

3. "There is more than enough room in my Father's house."

This is a beautiful promise for every one of us. We're not going to be in cramped accommodations, sleeping on our parents' sofa, crashing with a friend, or told there's no more room. There will be plenty of room for every single one of us. Have you ever tried to book a hotel room when the final flight out of an airport was canceled? That happened to me one night in Charlotte, North Carolina. Due to ice and snow, every flight was canceled until the following morning, stranding everyone at the airport. I called all the hotels close to the airport, but the message was the same, "Fully booked." That will never happen in heaven. There is room for us. As William Barclay declares, "Heaven is as wide as the heart of God."[2]

4. "If this were not so, would I have told you that I am going to prepare a place for you?"

Jesus never sugarcoated his words. He never pretended that the Christian life was going to be easy. In Matthew's Gospel Jesus told his followers, "If any of you wants to be my follower, you must give up your own way, take up your cross, and follow me" (Matt. 16:24). He never recruited his followers with promises of a smooth path but made it clear that suffering would be part of the journey. Everything he told his friends without exception was true. Now he is saying, you have my word, I'm going to prepare a place for you.

The word *place* used in this sentence (in the Greek language, *topos*) literally refers to a place that can be located, a real place. Heaven is not some ethereal space where we all float around for eternity. It is a real place where we will live with Jesus forever. Every human heart aches to belong, to be known, to be welcomed, to be expected. That's exactly what Jesus has prepared for you and for me, and we'll get there in his perfect timing and be expected by him.

Have you ever arrived a little early for a party or a dinner and you realize that they're not quite ready for you? It's embarrassing watching through the window as they stuff socks behind cushions and toss magazines behind the couch. Don't ask me how I know this!

That's not how heaven will be. He's prepared a place where you're expected, it's perfect, and everything is ready for you.

5. "I will come and get you, so that you will always be with me where I am."

This we can stake our lives on. Jesus is coming back again. This time not as a vulnerable baby but as King of Kings and Lord of Lords. Jesus promises us that when it's time he'll come for us so that we can live with him forever. When we pass from this life into the next, I imagine for the first time in our lives we will breathe out one word with every cell in our body, "Home!" and we will understand the weight of that word for the very first time. What a promise! Jesus has promised that he will come, he will personally come for you. Not only that, but you will be with him forever. Where he is, you will be.

Have you ever noticed that there's a little something wrong with everything down here? You're grateful for your home, but there's that one pesky neighbor. Your car's great, but there's a ding on the passenger side door. You're in the job you always wanted and it's good, but sometimes you wonder if you should have taken a different path. You take care of your body, but you have a bit of a twinge in your right knee. There's just a little something wrong with everything. That's because earth is not our home. We are just passing through. So let me assure you, in the Father's house, there's nothing wrong with anything.

How many homes have you lived in over the years? I've lived in over ten. I've lived in student housing, apartments, larger homes, and now our townhome. We're considering moving now, and not because of our ongoing reality show mentioned earlier but to move closer to friends and where we both work. But when I look around at all the stuff we've accumulated over the years, I cannot imagine moving; the thought is not appealing. Do you know that when we're finally home with Jesus we don't have to move anymore? (Our final glorious move will be in a new heaven and new earth; more about that later in another chapter.) We'll be living in our eternal home, perfectly made for us and prepared for us by Jesus, and we will be with him forever.

I have a sweet memory with my son from years ago when I was doing arena speaking tours with five other friends. Because of the size of the crowds, everyone had to have a backstage pass to get through security to catering. My son was young at the time, and his nanny was bringing him over to eat dinner with us. They were a little late, so I went to look for them and saw his darling nanny and Christian trying to convince the security guard that they were supposed to be allowed in, but they had forgotten their passes. The moment Christian saw me, he yelled out, "I'm with her. That's my mom." That will be my cry when I get home. "I'm with Jesus!" The great news is that when we are finally home, we won't need a pass, we'll be recognized immediately, and we'll be expected. I can't imagine what that will be like—finally home with Jesus.

We're Not Home Yet

The thought of home brings happy memories for me. As a student in seminary, it meant boarding a train in London for the five-hour trip north to Glasgow, then on to Ayr on the west coast. After I moved to America, it meant looking out the window as I flew back home at field after field of white, fluffy sheep as we were about to land in Scotland. My memories of home as I think back now are of my mum in her green chair by the fireplace, always there to welcome us home from school every day. Although we faced so much pain after the death of my father, my mum was a constant source of love and stability, always praying for her children.

The idea of going home is not always a welcome one. You might be divorced and the place you once called home is no longer home to you. It reminds you of what once was and what fell apart and hurt you so badly. But let me say this, when Jesus talked about home, about his Father's home, it was more than you and I have ever imagined in our wildest dreams. That can be a challenging picture to hold on to. Life is shifting all the time. It's hard to keep focused on what's waiting for us when so much of life on this earth is hard and disappointing. I think that's why heaven is mentioned in the Bible so many times, to remind us that we're not home yet. There are so many things to distract us, and we're encouraged to choose to remember who we are and where we belong. Can you imagine how beautiful our new lives will be? There will be no more fear, anxiety, comparison, jealousy, or insecurity because we'll finally be home. I can only imagine.

I want us to meditate on these verses one more time.

> Since you have been raised to new life with Christ, set your sights on the realities of heaven, where Christ sits in the place of honor at God's right hand. Think about the things of heaven, not the things of earth. (Col. 3:1–2)

We're not home yet—life still has its struggles—but because of Jesus, we have been raised to a brand-new life. This is our ultimate hope, so we set our sights on the realities of heaven.

Jesus Gave Us a Guarantee

I was brought up in church, so I've known and trusted in the story about Jesus's life, death, and resurrection for most of my life. But recently I had an experience that made everything so real, so present for me. I was in Israel filming a ten-week series on walking in the footsteps of Jesus. It was my first trip to Israel, and I found it very moving. I loved taking a little boat out on the Sea of Galilee, which was as still as glass that day. I stood on the Mount of Olives and looked down the Kidron Valley to the garden of Gethsemane and over to the old city of Jerusalem. But there was one day in particular that has left a profound imprint on my heart. On that day, I walked a winding road known as the Via Dolorosa, which translates as "the Way of Suffering." It's the road that Jesus took on the day he was executed.

The road was long and narrow and very busy that day, just as it would have been when Jesus took it, forced by the Roman soldiers on the way to his crucifixion. The route begins at the place where Christians believe Pilate condemned Jesus to death and ends at the Church of the Holy Sepulchre, which is believed to hold the tomb where Jesus was buried. I didn't expect the road to be so long or crowded. I stopped at several Stations of the Cross, places marking where Jesus fell, where he encountered his mother, and where Simon, a visitor from Libya, was forced to carry Jesus's cross, as he was so weak and had lost so much blood. We walked all the way to the place believed to be where he was crucified between two criminals, and finally where his body was laid in a borrowed tomb. It had been a long day of filming, and as the sun was setting over Jerusalem, I found a quiet place to sit and look over the old city. Jesus walked the same ancient limestone paths that I slipped and fell on that day, and I

> When we know Jesus, we have a guarantee that we will spend forever in heaven, a place prepared for us by him.

was overwhelmed by all he did for us. He did it all because he loves us. He did it all because he wanted us to finally make our way home to the place we were created for before everything went so wrong in the garden of Eden.

I don't want to assume that because you picked up a book on heaven you have a personal relationship with Jesus. You might simply be curious about what happens to us when we die, which I think many of us are. But Jesus took that road so that when you and I place our trust in him we can be absolutely, 100 percent sure that when we die, we're going to live in a new heaven and a new earth with him forever. Many people are afraid of dying, but we don't have to be. When we know Jesus, we have a guarantee that we will spend forever in heaven, a place prepared for us by him.

It was our first morning home from Israel and the radio was blaring outside our balcony. Then someone changed the station to play old gospel classics. Maggie still managed to muster up a couple of random barks, but when a familiar song came on, I went out on the balcony and joined in. I knew the words to this one. Perhaps you do too?

When we all get to heaven,
what a day of rejoicing that will be!
When we all see Jesus,
we'll sing and shout the victory![3]

Father God,

Thank you for sending Jesus to pay a price we could never pay so that we can live with you forever. I ask that by the power of your Holy Spirit, you would give me a passion and a thirst for heaven, my forever home.

In Jesus's powerful name,

Amen.

What I Know about Heaven

Heaven is a real place where I will live in a home prepared for me by Jesus, forever.

2

WHAT IS HEAVEN LIKE?

The heavens proclaim the glory of God.
    The skies display his craftsmanship.
Day after day they continue to speak;
    night after night they make him known.
They speak without a sound or word;
    their voice is never heard.

Psalm 19:1–3

M y father-in-law, William, moved in with us when Eleanor, my mother-in-law, died. He was seventy-nine years old. Our son was three years old at the time, and for him, having his papa under the same roof was like Christmas 365 days of the year. William allowed Christian to do things I never would, like putting an entire packet of gum in his mouth at once. A perfect gift to a three-year-old boy. William has been gone for several years now, but as I sit at my desk and think about our years together, it makes me laugh. He was a character on several fronts.

He didn't like to be alone, and he went everywhere with us. When we took a family vacation to Florida, his only concern was, "Do I have to be in a room of my own or can I share with y'all?" We got a bigger room.

When a small moving truck delivered his most precious belongings from his home in Charleston, South Carolina, to our home in Nashville at the time, he wanted to know if he could keep his best hammer and screwdriver with our knives and forks. Well, of course!

When we ate at a restaurant, he would wink at Christian halfway through the meal and they would take off dancing round the table doing a dance known only to them. They called it "the butt dance." I'll leave the rest to your imagination.

He also stretched the boundaries of medical science. A friend was staying overnight with us when she realized that she was on the verge of a severe urinary tract infection. This was fairly common for her, and very painful if she didn't nip it in the bud. She needed a prescription, but it was late in the evening and her doctor's office was closed. William decided to call a friend of his who was a doctor, but rather than ask for help for our friend, he said he needed it for himself. I could hear the doctor on the other end of the phone telling him that men don't usually get urinary tract infections, to which he replied, "I know they don't, but I've got one!" So he wasn't just a character . . . he was a rascal, and we enjoyed every minute of it.

One night William had gone downstairs to have a bath, and when he came back into the kitchen his head was covered in plaster and dust, and he was absolutely soaked. "Dad! What happened?" I asked. "Well," he said in his southern drawl, "all I can tell you is that this all came from the third heaven." Further investigation revealed that a pipe on the third floor had burst, water came through to the second floor, and brought William's ceiling over the bath on the bottom floor down on his head. Fortunately, he wasn't hurt, but we ended up later having an interesting discussion about the fact that there actually is a third heaven.

Heaven Is Up

When you hear that phrase "the third heaven," what comes to your mind? Do you think there is such a place? For William, he simply meant the third floor of our home, but the Bible makes it clear that there are indeed three "heavens."

1. The first heaven is the earth's atmosphere. It's what you see when you look out the window of an airplane. It's the home of birds and all flying creatures.

    "The rain and snow come down from the heavens and stay on the ground to water the earth" (Isa. 55:10).

2. The second heaven is outer space, where the stars and the multitude of planets and galaxies exist. We read about the creation of the second heaven in Genesis 1.

    "Then God said, 'Let lights appear in the sky to separate the day from the night. Let them be signs to mark the seasons, days, and years. Let these lights in the sky shine down on the earth.' And that is what happened. God made two great lights—the larger one to govern the day, and the smaller one to govern the night. He also made the stars. God set these lights in the sky to light the earth, to govern the day and night, and to separate the light from the darkness. And God saw that it was good" (vv. 14–18).

3. The third heaven is where God is right now; it's where his presence is. The Bible calls this simply *heaven* or *paradise*. The apostle Paul experienced this heaven.

    "I was caught up to the third heaven fourteen years ago. Whether I was in my body or out of my body, I don't know—only God knows. Yes, only God knows whether I was in my body or outside my body. But I do know that I was caught up to paradise and heard things so astounding that they cannot be expressed in words, things no human is allowed to tell" (2 Cor. 12:2–4).

Paul was *caught up*. When Christ ascended back to his Father, he went up!

In the book of Acts, Luke records Christ's ascension into heaven like this:

> After saying this, he was taken up into a cloud while they were watching, and they could no longer see him. As they strained to see him rising into heaven, two white-robed men suddenly stood among them. "Men of Galilee," they said, "why are you standing here staring into heaven? Jesus has been taken from you into heaven, but someday he will return from heaven in the same way you saw him go!" (1:9–11)

Just as the disciples saw Christ go, the promise is that he will return.

Heaven Is with Jesus

The thief crucified beside Jesus experienced this heaven.

> But the other criminal protested, "Don't you fear God even when you have been sentenced to die? We deserve to die for our crimes, but this man hasn't done anything wrong." Then he said, "Jesus, remember me when you come into your Kingdom."
>
> And Jesus replied, "I assure you, today you will be with me in paradise." (Luke 23:40–43)

This is one of the most amazing stories in the New Testament. We don't know anything about this man's life before he encountered Christ being crucified beside him. We know he was a criminal and his crime demanded the death penalty, not a lesser punishment. He had made peace with the fact that he was being executed and deserved to die. He was in the last hours of his life. If there was ever a moment in human history when being in the right place at the right time occurred, surely this was it. Can you imagine what it must have been like to turn your head and realize that you are being executed beside the Son of God? He didn't ask Jesus if he had any pull with the authorities on this earth; he recognized a far greater authority, Christ's kingdom. Jesus's response to him is staggering.

He didn't tell him it was a little too late.

He didn't ask him if he'd ever done anything good, anything redeemable.

He didn't ask him if he'd ever gone to temple.

No. He said this: "Today you will be with me in paradise" (Luke 23:43).

If you have ever wondered if the things you've done in your past are too great a weight for you to know the love and forgiveness of God, this story has got to clear that up. All the man did was cry out to Jesus and he was heading home forever.

Heaven Is Our Real Home

Jesus didn't tell this man that at some point in the future he would be with him. No, he said today you will be *not just in* paradise but *with me in paradise*.

Paul, writing to the church in Corinth sometime later, made it crystal clear that the moment we are gone from our body we are with the Lord.

> So we are always confident, even though we know that as long as we live in these bodies we are not at home with the Lord. For we live by believing and not by seeing. Yes, we are fully confident, and we would rather be away from these earthly bodies, for then we will be at home with the Lord. (2 Cor. 5:6–8)

Paul's message is unambiguous: to be absent from the body is to be at home with the Lord. That is the very definition of good news. Let me ask you a question: What do you believe will happen to you the moment you die? Have you ever wondered that? Do you think you simply stay in the ground until Jesus returns? Do you imagine that you might be in some disembodied limbo until the final resurrection? Scripture makes it clear that while our body stays in the ground, our spirit and soul go to be with Jesus in heaven. So when

> **To be absent from the body is to be at home with the Lord.**

I think about my family, that's where my mum and dad and grandparents are. Based on their relationship with Jesus before they died, their earthly bodies are in the ground waiting for their new resurrection bodies, but their spirits and souls are in the presence of the Lord. That's the same for you as well. All your loved ones who have placed their trust in Jesus are there now, with the Lord, experiencing joy and peace. As the psalmist wrote, "In Your presence is fullness of joy" (Ps. 16:11 AMP).

Let me show you another example from Scripture that illustrates this truth. This is one of my favorite stories in the Bible.

You may remember a young follower of Jesus who was stoned to death because he accused the religious leaders of his day of not realizing that Jesus was in fact the promised Messiah. His name was Stephen. The account of his final moments, although brutal in terms of human suffering, is triumphant in the reality of what is true for every one of us who has a relationship with Jesus.

> The Jewish leaders were infuriated by Stephen's accusation, and they shook their fists at him in rage. But Stephen, full of the Holy Spirit, gazed steadily into heaven and saw the glory of God, and he saw Jesus standing in the place of honor at God's right hand. And he told them, "Look, I see the heavens opened and the Son of Man standing in the place of honor at God's right hand!"

Then they put their hands over their ears and began shouting. They rushed at him and dragged him out of the city and began to stone him. His accusers took off their coats and laid them at the feet of a young man named Saul.

As they stoned him, Stephen prayed, "Lord Jesus, receive my spirit." (Acts 7:54–59)

Three things about this account are deeply moving to me.

1. When Stephen was surrounded by those who hated him, an angry religious crowd, he was able to gaze into heaven and see the glory of God. This was a gift given to Stephen. I often wonder how many of those who are being martyred for their faith even now are given that same beautiful gift.
2. Jesus was standing. This courageous young man received a standing ovation from Christ himself. There is nothing on this earth that could ever come close to that. Depending on what our lives look like, we all have things that seem to be the height of accomplishment—a promotion, an award, a title. Those would all fade into nothing compared to seeing Jesus waiting to welcome us home.
3. Stephen prayed, "Lord Jesus, receive my spirit." He knew his body would go into the ground but his spirit was about to be united with Jesus. Stephen was going home.

Heaven Is Comforting for Those Left Behind

On a deeply personal note, this understanding that those who die in Christ are immediately in his presence has brought me great comfort and healing. My dad had a brain aneurysm and a stroke when he was thirty-three years old. The damage to his brain resulted in major changes to his physical ability and his personality. He remained paralyzed down his left side until his death the following year and never regained his ability to speak. In terms of personality, he went from being a loving, fun dad, passionately committed to Jesus, to an angry, confused, and ultimately violent stranger. He was placed in a psychiatric institution when he was thirty-four. I can't fathom what he must have gone through in his more lucid moments because although he couldn't speak, my mum told me that he would often sit with his head in his hands and weep, aware of what had happened to the life he once knew. Several times he managed to escape the hospital grounds and make his way home, only to be returned again and again. On his final escape, he didn't try to come home anymore. He made his way to the river where he drowned himself.

There was little understanding of or empathy for mental illness in Scotland in those days. My dad was buried in an unmarked grave, and we left our village to start again in the town where my mum was born. We carried on as if nothing had happened. There was no therapy or family counseling in those days. Even if that option had been available, I don't think we would have taken it. We've never been very good at talking about hard things in our family. We just move on. But I've always struggled with just moving on. I felt as though we abandoned my dad. He had a hard childhood and such a short life, yet as I've studied about heaven in greater depth, I find tangible hope has taken the place of sadness. The moment my dad took his last breath on earth, he took his first in the presence of Jesus. He was finally safe; he was home.

I hope that gives you some comfort if you have had to say goodbye to a loved one who has suffered. It's one of the hardest things in this life to reconcile with our belief in a good and loving God. Other than the understanding that we are living on a fallen earth, I have no great wisdom on the presence of so much suffering in this world. What I do know though is that for those who have placed their trust in Christ, the joy of being with him eternally will far outweigh this present darkness.

It makes me think of that beautiful saying by Julian of Norwich, "All shall be well, and all shall be well and all manner of thing shall be well."[1]

Heaven Is Where We'll Be Fully Known at Last

I was born with blue-black hair like a raven's feathers. Over the years I've had several ill-advised experiments with coloring my own hair, and according to my hairstylist, I no longer have a "natural" color. Now, in an attempt to cover the rapidly encroaching gray, I've settled on light brown with blonde highlights. My family and friends all know me that way, all except for my aunt Mary. I was particularly fond of her growing up. She has been gone for several years now, but when I knew her, she was a fiercely independent Scottish woman who lived alone after the death of my uncle. She would get down on her knees every Saturday morning and polish her front doorstep with cardinal red polish until it shone. She'd dig up her own potatoes from her vegetable garden, and she always had a fire burning in the hearth. I loved visiting her on trips back home to Scotland. If she knew she had visitors coming, she was up at dawn baking scones and cakes and pies. She loved having visitors and regaled us all with tales of life in Scotland when she was a child, which is why it was a little strange to me that she seemed to be trying to get me out of the door on one visit after only two cups of tea, a scone, and a slice of her famous rhubarb pie. Finally, she said in her trademark Scottish brogue, "I'm sorry to ask you to leave, lassie, but my niece Sheila is coming to see me all the way from America, so she'll be wanting a cup of tea."

"Aunt Mary," I said. "It's me, I'm Sheila."

"Never!" she said, clearly shocked. "What happened to your hair? I wouldn't have recognized you if you'd jumped out of my porridge!"

I laughed about that for a while, but let's think about it.

Will we recognize each other in heaven? What will we look like? Will we look the same as we did on earth?

Let me say up front that I firmly believe we will recognize and know each other in heaven. There are several passages and stories in Scripture that support that belief. Not only that, but I believe we'll recognize godly men and women who died long before us. You may remember this passage from Mark's Gospel.

Six days later Jesus took Peter, James, and John, and led them up a high mountain to be alone. As the men watched, Jesus' appearance was transformed, and his clothes became dazzling white, far whiter than any earthly bleach could ever make them. Then Elijah and Moses appeared and began talking with Jesus.

Peter exclaimed, "Rabbi, it's wonderful for us to be here! Let's make three shelters as memorials—one for you, one for Moses, and one for Elijah." He said this because he didn't really know what else to say, for they were all terrified.

Then a cloud overshadowed them, and a voice from the cloud said, "This is my dearly loved Son. Listen to him." Suddenly, when they looked around, Moses and Elijah were gone, and they saw only Jesus with them. (Mark 9:2–8)

Have you ever wondered how the disciples recognized Moses and Elijah? This was long before photographs and magazines. We get a clue from Matthew's Gospel. In chapter 17 he shares the same story of that transfiguration on the mountaintop, but one chapter earlier he helps us understand where Peter's perception came from. It's just a few days before Jesus will ride into Jerusalem on a colt and begin the countdown to the events leading up to his crucifixion. Jesus asks his friends what people are saying about who he is. They tell him that some people think he is Elijah, the prophet, or one of the other prophets from the Old Testament. Then Jesus asks a critical question.

Then he asked them, "But who do you say I am?"

Simon Peter answered, "You are the Messiah, the Son of the living God."

Jesus replied, "You are blessed, Simon son of John, because my Father in heaven has revealed this to you. You did not learn this from any human being." (Matt. 16:15–17)

God himself revealed Christ's identity to Peter. The Holy Spirit gave him understanding. God gave Peter eyes to recognize Moses and Elijah just as he had to recognize Jesus, but the fact remains, they were recognizable as people, as two men standing talking with Jesus. I can't imagine what it must have been like to see Jesus like that. Since his birth, his glory had been concealed, but in this moment on the mountain peak of Mount Horeb, Jesus's face and his clothes became as brilliant as the sun. We're not given ears into that conversation between Jesus, Moses, and Elijah, but I can only imagine how critical that was as Jesus prepared for the days ahead. Moses represented the law that was given to God's people, and Elijah represented all the prophetic line that led up to that moment when Christ was born in Bethlehem. This was the culmination of the heart of the Old Testament. Christ was the fulfillment of the law and the One promised through the prophets. He was the One whose story was woven through every page of the Old Testament, from Genesis to the four hundred years of God's silence as the Old Testament closed. Now, in Christ, grace and truth came together.

Then the ultimate voice, God the Father, spoke: "This is my dearly loved Son, who brings me great joy. Listen to him" (Matt. 17:5).

We know that God's voice was heard when Jesus was baptized (Luke 3:21–22), but we don't know if Christ heard his Father's audible voice again until that day on the mountaintop. If we are allowed to imagine, I think Moses and Elijah would have encouraged Jesus that he was exactly where he should be, the good plan from the beginning of time was in place, and he was ready.

Heaven Gives Us Glorified Bodies

I overheard a funny conversation between a grandmother and her granddaughter one day as I was leaving church. She was trying to explain to the little girl what a glorified body in heaven would look like. The little girl was quiet for a moment and then asked, "Do you think we'll all look like Barbie?"

Well, hallelujah, I'm pretty sure none of us will look like Barbie. You will look like you and I'll look like me. Will our bodies look like our human bodies? Absolutely! One thing we know for sure, there will be at least three real bodies in heaven that look like they did on earth—Jesus, Elijah, and Enoch because they were taken up—but they will be supercharged.

Jesus—We know that when Jesus appeared to his friends after his resurrection, he had a real body with some changes. He was able to cook and share a meal with them beside the Sea of Galilee (John 21:1–14). He invited Thomas to touch the wounds in his hands and side (20:24–29). But his body had new properties in that he could suddenly appear in a room without opening a door and was able to disappear just as he had appeared (v. 19).

Elijah—Elijah was one of two men in the Old Testament who never died a physical death on the earth.

> As they were walking along and talking, suddenly a chariot of fire appeared, drawn by horses of fire. It drove between the two men, separating them, and Elijah was carried by a whirlwind into heaven. (2 Kings 2:11)

It was the end of Elijah's ministry and time for Elisha, his disciple, to take over. If you read the full story in 2 Kings 2, it's clear what Elisha wanted from his master. In those days it was common for the firstborn son in a family to receive a double portion of the family money as an inheritance. However, Elisha—Elijah's spiritual son—

didn't want money. He wanted a double portion of the power of God in Elijah's life. Elijah clearly knew that he was going to be taken up into heaven, and he told Elisha that if he caught sight of him leaving, then his request would be granted. What a sight that must have been as a chariot of fire appeared racing between and separating the two men as Elijah was carried by a whirlwind into heaven. Interestingly enough, Elijah performed eight miracles in his life, and Elisha performed sixteen.

Enoch—We don't know very much about Enoch apart from this reference in Genesis and a further one in Hebrews.

> When Enoch was 65 years old, he became the father of Methuselah. After the birth of Methuselah, Enoch lived in close fellowship with God for another 300 years, and he had other sons and daughters. Enoch lived 365 years, walking in close fellowship with God. Then one day he disappeared, because God took him. (Gen. 5:21–24)

He's included in the great faith chapter, Hebrews 11.

> It was by faith that Enoch was taken up to heaven without dying—"he disappeared, because God took him." For before he was taken up, he was known as a person who pleased God. (Heb. 11:5)

That one verse in Genesis actually tells us quite a lot about Enoch. After his son Methuselah was born, we read that he lived in "close fellowship with God" for another three hundred years. For his day and time, that speaks volumes about the man he was. To walk closely with God is the commitment of a lifetime, not the decision of a moment. It's daily living out the faith on the best days, and the worst. It's to keep walking with God when your prayers get answered

> **To walk closely with God is the commitment of a lifetime, not the decision of a moment.**

41

and when it seems as if they go no higher than the ceiling. I want to live as Enoch did, to walk closely with God every single day. In my mind I imagine Enoch walking and talking with God every day, and then one day God says, "Enoch, we're closer to my house now than yours. Let's go home!"

We know for sure there will be at least three real human bodies in heaven, but I believe that we will all have a body even though it won't be our final resurrected body. Paul makes it pretty clear in his letter to the church in Corinth.

> For we know that when this earthly tent we live in is taken down (that is, when we die and leave this earthly body), we will have a house in heaven, an eternal body made for us by God himself and not by human hands. We grow weary in our present bodies, and we long to put on our heavenly bodies like new clothing. For we will put on heavenly bodies; we will not be spirits without bodies. (2 Cor. 5:1–3)

We will not be floating around on a cloud. We will have real, though changed, bodies, ones that will not grow tired.

Heaven Is Not Boring

I have to admit that as a young Christian I worried about heaven being boring. Clearly heaven was to be preferred over the alternative, but what would we do all the time? Would it be like one long, never-ending, continuous church service? At one point I remember asking my mum if it would be possible to be buried with a stack of books just to have a little reading material.

Heaven will not be boring for one simple reason: God is not boring. Life can be boring, but God is not boring. He never has been and never will be. If we fall into the trap of believing that heaven will be boring, we've bought into the very first lie that caused humans' downfall. If you think about the life that Adam and Eve enjoyed in

Eden, it was perfect. If you're unfamiliar with it, you can read about it in Genesis 2. They loved each other. They loved God and walked and talked with him in the cool of each evening. There was no shame, no jealousy, no pain, no tears, no competition, no weariness, no sadness, no depression, no aging, and no sickness. They lived in an unspeakably beautiful place. "The LORD God made all sorts of trees grow up from the ground—trees that were beautiful and that produced delicious fruit. In the middle of the garden he placed the tree of life and the tree of the knowledge of good and evil" (v. 9).

Adam got to name every animal and every bird, and they all lived at peace with one another. God saw that Adam was still lonely, and so he created Eve from one of Adam's ribs. "'At last!' the man exclaimed. 'This one is bone from my bone, and flesh from my flesh!'" (v. 23).

It's hard to paint a picture of Eden because inevitably we'll compare it to what we know, and what we know now doesn't begin to compare to what they once knew. What was this first lie that shattered the world?

God's holding out on you!
There's so much more than what you have here.
This is boring; just try the fruit from that tree over there.

And so they did, and here we are.

Interestingly that will be Satan's lie at the end of the age as his time is running out. He will lie and blaspheme against God and those who dwell with him in heaven. In the revelation given to John the apostle on the Isle of Patmos, this is what he saw: "And he spoke terrible words of blasphemy against God, slandering his name and his dwelling—that is, those who dwell in heaven" (Rev. 13:6).

The enemy hates all God loves, and that's you and me. He will do all he can to encourage us to live distracted lives on earth so that the thought of continuing that eternally will have no appeal. He is the consummate liar.

The Wonder of Heaven

There is such an urgency in my heart for us to wake up. To wake up to the lies of the enemy and to remain faithful to Christ, the One who gave everything to bring us back from the broken beauty of the garden, home again. Here on earth, even in the best moments, we barely have a glimpse of the wonder of heaven. It's everything you've ever dreamt of in its purest form and so much more. If we don't know Jesus, when we're not in relationship with the One who created us, then it's easy to believe that there is nothing more than what we know now. When you've grabbed hold of everything this world offers and found it heartbreakingly wanting, it's easy to give in to despair. I've seen it up close with friends, and I've watched it from a distance.

British actor George Sanders tried everything to make himself happy. He had four wives, tried seven psychiatrists, appeared in more than ninety films, and won an Oscar for his role in one of my favorite movies, *All about Eve*. Yet on April 25, 1972, at age sixty-five, Sanders took his own life and left behind this suicide note.

> Dear World, I am leaving because I am bored. I feel I have lived long enough. I am leaving you with your worries in this sweet cesspool. Good luck.[2]

So sad. Such a lie that this is all that God intended for us, and if we buy into it, we forget who God the creative Mastermind is. I love how Randy Alcorn puts it:

> We think of ourselves as fun-loving and of God as a humorless killjoy. But we've got it backward. It's not God who's boring, it's us. Did we

invent wit, humor, and laughter? No, God did. We'll never begin to exhaust God's sense of humor and his love for adventure. The real question is this: How could God not be bored with *us*?[3]

But he's not. I promise you that you and I have not even begun to understand what real joy, laughter, adventure, exhilaration, and wonder are. I'm only at the beginning of writing this book and I could dance. And there's so much more!

Father God,
Thank you for loving me so much that you made it possible for me to be with Jesus in heaven the moment I die. Thank you that there will be joy and I'll see my loved ones who know you once more.
Amen.

What I Know about Heaven

When we die, we will immediately go to heaven to
be with Jesus where there is fullness of joy.

3

WILL HEAVEN HEAL OUR DISAPPOINTMENTS?

Sometimes we can hardly wait to move—and so we cry out in frustration.
Compared to what's coming, living conditions around here seem like a
stopover in an unfurnished shack, and we're tired of it! We've been given
a glimpse of the real thing, our true home, our resurrection bodies! The
Spirit of God whets our appetite by giving us a taste of what's ahead.
He puts a little of heaven in our hearts so that we'll never settle for less.

2 Corinthians 5:2–4 MSG

Growing up in Scotland close to the ocean, I would walk for
miles along the edge of the seashore or across the hills when
they were brilliant with yellow gorse bushes and purple
heather. Some days it felt like a little taste of heaven. Walking is
good for my mental health. When life feels overwhelming or too
complicated, I walk. This daily routine morphed into something a
lot less peaceful when Maggie, our Yorkie, joined our family. Let me
say up front in her defense that she is a darling dog; we love her so

much. But as I mentioned earlier, she has one predominant problem: she is a barker. She barks, not simply when someone comes to the door, she barks at everything and everyone on our morning walks. You may have heard of the *Dog-Whisperer*; well, I have become the *Dog-Apologizer*. It's a disaster. I've tried taking her early in the morning hoping not to bump into other people walking their dogs, but it's pointless. We live in Dallas, Texas, a busy metropolis, and there is always someone else out walking their well-behaved dogs, big and small. My mornings sound a bit like this:

"So sorry. She's a good dog, really."
"I am so sorry. She's just saying hello."
"Sorry! No, she won't bite you."

I've even resorted to made-up tales.

"Her mother was a street fighter."
"She was traumatized by a bull as a puppy."
"I think there's a storm coming. She's warning us. Hurry inside!"

All in all, it's a disaster. I've worked with trainers. I've tried the coin-in-a-can trick and spraying her with water (I refuse to use the bark collar), but she seems to enjoy them all. So my daily source of peace and quiet has turned into a three-ring circus.

Then one day I saw an advertisement online that seemed to offer me the hope I longed for. It was a four-week training camp, on a farm, for dogs. The ad promised that they would curb barking, socialize your dog with other dogs and horses, and train them to be the pet you have always wanted. We've never bumped into a horse on our walks but she does tend to view big dogs as fair game, so I thought, big dog, small horse, same thing. I hesitated initially as it was quite expensive, but the idea that they promised they could train Maggie not to bark at everyone was too good to pass up. I read the reviews online, and each one sang the praises of the miracles that had taken place in the lives of their dogs when they came home. So we signed up. The farm was a couple of hours outside of Dallas, but they even came and picked Maggie up. They told us that they would post pictures and videos every day so that we could see her progress. I remember waving goodbye and all I could hear was that familiar bark as they drove off down the street. *No more*, I thought.

The first few videos weren't very encouraging, but I reasoned, "It's early still. She's got three more weeks." Every day I'd go to the website and look at the videos of all the other dogs running merrily across the fields, playing together and being introduced to the horses, and there was Maggie bringing up the rear barking like a nut. By the third week, she wasn't even in the videos anymore. She was sitting in a tractor with the farmer. When I called to ask what was going on, the response was, "She's not very good with other dogs."

"Yes . . . that was kind of the point," I replied.

They returned her four weeks later, and I could hear her barking from two streets away. All I longed for was a little peace and quiet, but, alas, no. I have resigned myself to the inevitable daily routine of neighbors crossing to the other side of the street when they see us coming. I no longer apologize, I just wave.

The dog trainers promised, but they just couldn't deliver.

When Nothing Feels Right

I think that's one of the most challenging issues when it comes to faith, to belief, to hope, to anticipating heaven. We live in a culture that promises so much and, more often than not, fails to deliver. It's hard not to become skeptical about everything.

Lose forty pounds in forty days!

Improve your golf swing in five easy lessons.

Look ten years younger with this miracle in a jar!

Grow your hair back in twenty-one days.

There is something in us, as if woven into our DNA, that believes that life should be better than we're experiencing right now. When I voiced my frustration with this world to myself, it felt very unspiritual and faithless to say, "I'm fed up with earth." Then I read Paul's second letter to the church in Corinth, and he shared the same thing.

> Sometimes we can hardly wait to move—and so we cry out in frustration. Compared to what's coming, living conditions around here seem like a stopover in an unfurnished shack, and we're tired of it! (2 Corinthians 5:1–2 MSG)

Do you ever feel like that, frustrated, unsettled? Are you tired of it all? You got the job you'd been hoping for. You found the husband or wife of your dreams. You work so hard to provide for your family. You take that anticipated vacation. You get your children into the right college or into a job that means they can finally pay their own bills. You do it all and yet you fall into bed each night and think, *Is this all there is?* If you feel that way, I want you to know you are not alone. This is not an unnatural feeling but a deep desire for what you were actually made for. It's as Frederick Buechner wrote, "Like Adam we have all lost paradise and yet we carry paradise around inside of us in the form of a longing for, almost a memory of, a blessedness that is no more, or the dream of a blessedness that may someday be again."[1]

C. S. Lewis wrote about similar frustrations in his classic work *Mere Christianity*. I read it for the first time when I was a teenager, but I reread it when our son was studying it in high school and understood it at a depth I never had before. Lewis was an English intellectual, a brilliant writer, and an Anglican lay theologian. He held academic positions in English literature at both Oxford University and Cambridge University, but the way he was able to write about this world and heaven has left such an imprint on my heart and soul. He "gets us." He put what he understood into books, and those books are on shelves where men and women like you and me can reach them. Lewis had a God-given ability to put our frustrations and questions into words that make sense.

In *Mere Christianity* Lewis unpacks three ways to deal with the disappointment, the restlessness that we inevitably face at times in life: fix it externally, fix it internally, or fix it eternally.[2]

Fix It Externally

Lewis calls the first "The Fool's Way." His premise is that fools think they simply haven't found the right thing yet. If they could just get a bigger house or a better car or a different husband or wife. The problems, the discontent are all external. Think about that. If we're being honest with ourselves, we've probably all been a little like that at times. The reason we don't like our job is because of that other employee. The reason that we want to find a new church is because the music is all wrong. The reason we're not happy in our marriage is because our spouse knows how to push our buttons. Now, if we have surrendered our lives to Christ, we can start in that place, but by his grace and with the help of the Holy Spirit we hopefully mature and learn to "own our own stuff." But that takes intentional work, it takes changing the way we think. For many who look for that "mysterious something" outside of a relationship with Christ, happiness is just the next elusive experience away. I think that's why we have so many unhappy people in the world today. Nothing is quite what they thought it would be.

I remember being invited some years ago to a party at a very well-known person's country estate. The only reason that I'd been invited was because I was hosting a show on British television at the time. I recognized almost everyone at the party but not because I knew them personally, simply because I knew who they were. They were some of the richest people, the most beautiful faces you see in magazines and on red carpets. I sat out by the pool in the clear night air wondering why I was there at all. What was clear to me as the evening progressed, however, was what seemed to lie just behind the perfect images. When they had consumed enough alcohol to loosen tongues and inhibitions, truth and unhappiness spilled out. I think it's a common belief that if we were really rich and famous, if we won the lottery, if we could buy anything we wanted without giving it a second thought, then we would know a new level of happiness, we could finally settle, it would be enough. But it never is. For many who have achieved these things, the golden box at the top of the ladder is disappointingly empty.

Fix It Internally

The next person Lewis identifies is what he calls "The Disillusioned," or "Sensible Man." He suggests that way of thinking is one that comes with age. One no longer expects big things or indulges crazy dreams. This is the man or woman who is sadly resigned to the fact that what he or she wanted out of life was simply the romanticism of a younger self, which was unrealistic and is never going to happen. I think many Christians have settled in this place. Life's not great, but it's not terrible. Your marriage doesn't bring you a lot of joy, but it's fine. You don't love your job, but you don't hate it and it pays the bills. That is a sad place to rest. It's better than blaming everything and everyone else for what's not working in life, but this is not what Jesus died to pay for. He did not shed his blood so that we could lose hope and simply bury the gifts, the dreams he's given us. Think about your life. What were the hopes and dreams you had when you were younger that you've simply let go of? Did you try them and it just didn't work out? Was the whole thing simply too much?

I imagine sitting down with you over a cup of coffee and you telling me the reasons why you gave up on certain things, and honestly, part of your argument would make perfect sense. The job you dreamt of did fall a bit short, the gifts you believed you had have never really been given the oxygen they needed, it's true. But then I'd ask you, what if they were not meant only for this world? What if they were a promise, a whisper of what's to come? What if every desire, hope, dream that's deep inside you is only the seed of what's to come into fruition eternally and perfectly? That is the heart of what Lewis identifies as the third way.

Fix It Eternally

He calls it "The Christian Way." He suggests that the deep aches that are never adequately met on this earth are for another place. Earthly pleasures were never supposed to fill all our emptiness but rather to point us to God, to wake our souls up. Earthly blessings are simply that. Rather than despise their failings, we accept them and keep our eyes turned toward our heavenly home.

I am grateful for these ideas expressed by Lewis. It gives us the perfect balance between hopelessness that this is all there is and denial, pretending that everything is fine when it's clearly not. Disappointment is real. It's part of our lives on this earth, but disappointment doesn't exist in heaven.

I have never in my life been more passionately excited about a growing understanding of and thirst for heaven. It's the kind of feeling you have when you've just been given some ridiculously good news and you can't wait to tell someone. Or the movie you've been waiting for months to see is finally here and you're in the theater waiting for the lights to go down. I don't know what you imagine when you think about heaven, but I promise you, whatever you can think up,

> **Disappointment doesn't exist in heaven.**

imagine, dream of won't compare to what God has prepared for you. Paul puts it this way:

> That is what the Scriptures mean when they say, "No eye has seen, no ear has heard, and no mind has imagined what God has prepared for those who love him." But it was to us that God revealed these things by his Spirit. For his Spirit searches out everything and shows us God's deep secrets. (1 Cor. 2:9–10)

I've listened to messages that focus only on the first part of that verse and use it as a reason to assume we can't know anything about heaven. They'll quote only this part: "No eye has seen, no ear has heard, and no mind has imagined what God has prepared for those who love him," and leave it there as if to say, *Then why even try?* I am not a fan of pulling part of a verse out of Scripture because when we lose the context, we lose the heart and the meaning of the text. In this case Paul goes on to say, "But it was to us that God revealed these things by his Spirit. For his Spirit searches out everything and shows us God's deep secrets."

Reasons Why You Should Be Excited about Heaven

God has revealed to us through his Son, through the Holy Spirit, and through Scripture so many reasons for why we should be excited about heaven. When we get to the chapter on a new heaven and a new earth later in the book, I believe that our minds will be blown. But for now let's look at a few reasons why we have so much to look forward to.

1. Jesus will be there.

This is the best news there is. Jesus will be there. I can't imagine what it will be like to finally see Jesus. To be able to kneel at his feet. To be able to look into his eyes and feel a love that nothing on earth has prepared us for. I think of friends of mine who are going through very hard things right now; perhaps you are there as well—cancer, divorce, struggling to pay your bills, chronic illness. Every day must feel like a battle. But I know for sure that the moment they, the moment you, look into Jesus's eyes, all the pain will be gone in a second. I've always thought that we'd cry when we first see Jesus, but now, I wonder if it's more likely that we'll laugh. Will we laugh with pure, unadulterated joy until tears run down our faces because every messy piece of our lives has fallen away? We'll be home and we'll be loved and we'll be whole and we will join in worshiping Christ, the Lamb of God, the King of Kings forever.

> And then I heard every creature in heaven and on earth and under the earth and in the sea. They sang: "Blessing and honor and glory and power belong to the one sitting on the throne and to the Lamb forever and ever." (Rev. 5:13)

It's hard to imagine what that day will be like as all human, earthbound restrictions will be gone. The picture that we currently have of Jesus will be radically transformed. Christ came in human flesh to show us what God the Father is like and to pay a debt we could never pay, and so we have human images of Jesus that we are familiar with. He ate with his friends, he wept, he walked for miles, he got tired, he laughed, he slept, he loved children, he loved people whom no one else would love, he saw us. I wonder sometimes if because we have those beautiful images of the humanity of Jesus, we forget who he really is in his eternal glory. He welcomes us to be familiar with him, but when we see him in heaven he will no longer be in fragile human form; he will be beyond glorious. This is the great eternal dichotomy that we will recognize him as our Savior, our Friend, and our Shepherd by the nail-pierced hands and side, and yet we will suddenly see all of who he has always been. Can you imagine?

I'm struggling here to find the words to even begin to describe how beautiful he is and how outrageously humble a Savior and Servant he is, that he would leave the multitudes in heaven who worship him day and night simply because he loves us. This is how Paul describes that beautiful deliberate descent:

> Think of yourselves the way Christ Jesus thought of himself. He had equal status with God but didn't think so much of himself that he had to cling to the advantages of that status no matter what. Not at all. When the time came, he set aside the privileges of deity and took on the status of a slave, became *human*! Having become human, he stayed human. It was an incredibly humbling process. He didn't claim special privileges. Instead, he lived a selfless, obedient life and then died a selfless, obedient death—and the worst kind of death at that—a crucifixion.
>
> Because of that obedience, God lifted him high and honored him far beyond anyone or anything, ever, so that all created beings in heaven and on earth—even those long ago dead and buried—will bow in worship before this Jesus Christ, and call out in praise that he is the Master of all, to the glorious honor of God the Father. (Phil. 2:5–11 MSG)

I love how the last three verses of that passage read in the New Living Translation.

> Therefore, God elevated him to the place of highest honor and gave him the name above all other names, that at the name of Jesus every knee should bow, in heaven and on earth and under the earth, and every tongue declare that Jesus Christ is Lord, to the glory of God the Father. (vv. 9–11)

I have a hard time reading that Scripture sitting down. When I get to "Therefore," I want to stand on a table and shout it out. The truth that Jesus loves you and me so much that he would come in this outrageous, unprecedented disguise and be brutally executed so that you and I can live in heaven with him forever makes me want to sing. It's too much to take in.

I've written before of almost losing my little West Highland white terrier, Charlie. But as time went on, I began to see in a fresh way how that very experience was a tiny glimpse, an imperfect picture of what Jesus did for us. Charlie had chased his favorite ball across the street. It had been raining and the road was slick and wet. I watched in horror as the ball rolled into the storm drain and my little dog followed it and disappeared as well. I broke all my nails trying to lift the metal plate that was on the sidewalk above the drain to try and reach him, but it was too heavy. I couldn't move it. I rang one of my neighbor's doorbells and asked if he could help me. He got a crowbar from his garage, and he and his teenage son were able to lift the metal plate. I could just see that Charlie was perched on a ledge about six feet down in the darkness. He was wet and shivering. I knew that if he slipped off that ledge, I would lose him. I had no idea what to do, but the dad had a plan. Thank God for dads. He told me that as his son was tall and thin, he was going to hold him by the ankles and lower him into the drain. I said to his son, "When you reach him, grab hold of him and don't let go. He might wriggle or bark or try to nip you, but please, just don't let go." This darling boy was able to return my sweet little Charlie to me.

I want you to imagine for a moment a scene in heaven. I'm clearly taking some license here, but the heart of the message is true. I imagine a moment when God the Father says to Christ the Son, "I'm going to lower you down into the darkness, and when you get there, hold on to them. They will wriggle and scream and bite you. Just don't let go." Christ responded, "Yes, Father."

For I have come down from heaven to do the will of God who sent me, not to do my own will. And this is the will of God, that I should

57

not lose even one of all those he has given me, but that I should raise them up at the last day. (John 6:38–39)

That's our Jesus. That's how much we are loved.

2. Your citizenship is there.

Not only will you finally see Jesus, but you will also be a citizen of heaven. You'll belong there. You're not visiting, your heavenly passport says, you are home, this is your country.

When I first came to America, I had a green card. It allowed me to live and work permanently in the United States. Then I married Barry and we had our son, Christian. So Barry and Christian had US passports and I had a United Kingdom passport. That was fine until we were watching a movie one day about a plane being hijacked. The hijackers separated the US passport holders from the rest of the passengers and made those who were not US citizens get off the plane. That's all it took. The next morning I began the process of becoming a US citizen. No one was going to be putting me off the plane, leaving my family behind. That's a far from perfect illustration, but what I want you to know is that when you are a citizen of heaven, you belong there; no one can or ever will ask you to leave.

But we are citizens of heaven, where the Lord Jesus Christ lives. (Phil. 3:20)

(On a lighter note, if you are ever in the position to take the oral test to become a US citizen, just a little heads-up. They do not have a sense of humor. When I was asked if I was willing to bear arms for my country, I told him that I've never looked good in a sleeveless blouse. Nothing. Zilch. Not a smirk. Nada.)

3. *Your friends and family are there.*

One of the most amazing things about being in heaven will be that we'll experience the greatest reunions we've ever known. We'll get to see friends and family who have trusted in Jesus and who've gone before us—and not as they were but as they are without any pain or sorrow, without anxiety or depression or any kind of sickness. There will be no fear or comparison, just overwhelming gratitude that we are finally home.

I have a photo I treasure of four generations of women, my great-grandmother, my grandmother, my mum, and my sister and me. My mum told me that my great-grandmother, who died when I was a baby, was the godliest woman she ever knew. She never once in her life heard her say an unkind word about anyone. Her response to difficult people was always, "We don't know what they might be going through." I can't wait to see her in heaven. I want to thank her for the life she lived, for the faith that carried her through the years, for all that she poured into my grandmother and how that legacy was passed down to my mum then to my sister and me.

I think of those of you who are lonely, who have lost a husband or a wife, a parent or a sibling—that is a hard weight to carry. When the loss is sudden, there's no time to prepare, no time to say the things you wanted to say. Our great hope, however, is that we will be together again.

I think of moms and dads who have lost children. That has to be the greatest heartache of all. I can't imagine that kind of pain. I have watched friends walk through this devastating loss. It is as if a part of them has been ripped out of their body and it's hard to even take a breath again. One of my friends who has lost two sons told me that when the pain is the freshest, words should be the fewest. At times like these all we can give each other is the gift of our presence and our love. The reunions that will take place in heaven between moms and dads and the children who have gone ahead of them must surely be the sweetest of all. You will see your little one again. (More on this in chapter 5.)

Even King David, Israel's greatest king, spoke of that day. In 2 Samuel we read about his adulterous affair with Bathsheba, the wife of one of his closest friends. Bathsheba became pregnant and gave birth to a son, but the baby was deathly ill. For days David refused to eat, to drink, to sleep. He lay on the floor and prayed that God would restore his son. His servants begged him to eat, but he refused until the little one died. Then he got up, dressed, and ate.

> "We don't understand you," they told him. "While the child was still living, you wept and refused to eat. But now that the child is dead, you have stopped your mourning and are eating again."
>
> David replied, "I fasted and wept while the child was alive, for I said, 'Perhaps the LORD will be gracious to me and let the child live.' But why should I fast when he is dead? Can I bring him back again? I will go to him one day, but he cannot return to me." (12:21–23)

David knew that his little one was safe in heaven and one day that sweet reunion would take place.

Only God knows the pain that you uniquely carry, and he is uniquely qualified to be your comforter.

> The Lord is close to the brokenhearted;
> he rescues those whose spirits are crushed. (Ps. 34:18)

4. Your spiritual heroes are there.

Not only will we be reunited with those we love who died before us, but we'll finally get to meet those we've read about, those whose lives have inspired and encouraged us. Can you imagine what it will be like to sit down with Moses, Elijah, Abraham, David, or Mary the mother of Jesus and simply know them as our brothers and sisters? I think it will be wonderful to chat with C. S. Lewis or Tolkien, with Amy Carmichael or Charles Spurgeon. I think I'm most looking forward to talking with John, the beloved disciple. I love the way he understood that Jesus loved him; it's

> **There will be one hero and one hero alone in heaven and his name is Jesus!**

sprinkled all through his Gospel account. He refers to himself in John 21:7 as "the disciple Jesus loved."

Think of all the people who have shaped your life, those in Scripture and those whose books you've read or stories you've heard. I think the greatest thing will be a vision correction, a fine-tuning of our focus. We tend to put certain people on pedestals and think that somehow they are spiritually superior to us, and while it's fine to be encouraged by a brother or sister, there will be one hero and one hero alone in heaven and his name is Jesus!

5. Peace and joy are finally yours forever.

I remember a day when I was still a little girl sitting on a towel on the beach beside my mum. It was an unusually warm spring day for Scotland. There was no wind, and the sea was like glass. The sky was periwinkle blue, and we could see across the water to the Isle of Arran. There was still a touch of snow on the peak of Goatfell, its tallest mountain. It was a perfect day. I asked my mum, "Do you think this is what heaven will be like?" "This and so much more," she said.

This and so much more. That's what heaven will be like. This and so much more.

The peace you've hoped for.

The joy you've prayed for.

The rest that you are weary for, as all disappointment is gone forever.

This and so much more.

Father,
Thank you that you have placed deep inside of me such a desire for everything you have prepared for me. Today, give me the grace to live in what is as I wait for what will be.
Amen.

What I Know about Heaven

Everything you are hoping for will be in heaven,
and you will finally know true peace and joy.

4

DOES EVERYONE
GO TO HEAVEN?

Jesus told him, "I am the way, the truth, and the life. No one can come
to the Father except through me."

John 14:6

It was our first spring break trip. We'd been on family vacations
before, but this was the inaugural "Woohoo, it's spring break from
school, let's party on" trip. Christian was nine years old, and the
thing he wanted to do more than anything else was learn to scuba dive
and ride a Jet Ski. I had (and continue to have) zero desire to scuba dive.
I've never recovered from watching *20,000 Leagues Under the Sea* with
the gigantic squid, or kraken, or whatever that disgusting sea-beast was
that wrapped its substantial self around Captain Nemo's submarine.
Also, as a Scot, I have a healthy regard for the Loch Ness or any other
monster that might suddenly surface to drag me to the bottom of
the murky waters never to be seen again. Barry, having never seen the
movie, said he was happy to learn to scuba dive, so we were good to go.

After doing a little research, we settled on Mexico, as it's close to
Texas and is known for excellent scuba diving and snorkeling. We

booked a nice family resort for the week and began to prepare for our trip. I made sure we had everything we'd need: sunscreen, sunglasses, bathing suits, hats, shorts, T-shirts, a camera, and a few good books for me. The resort assured us they would provide the necessary scuba gear. But for some reason, which eludes me now, I wasn't sure if Christian would need a passport at age nine. I called our airline to check. A very helpful woman named Blanche assured me that he would not need a passport so, as Barry and I already had ours, we were set. We took a cab to the airport that morning and got in line behind all the other excited spring-breakers checking in for their trips.

"Mom, when we get to the hotel can we go straight to the beach?" Christian asked.

"Absolutely," I assured him. "We'll open our hotel room, throw our cases in, and head right to the water."

Soon it was our turn, and Barry presented our identification.

"Can I have your son's passport?" the agent asked.

"He doesn't need one," Barry said. "He's just nine."

"No, he needs a passport, sir," he said.

Barry had a look of panic as he turned to me.

"It's okay," I said. "I've got this."

I turned to the agent. "Hello, sir. I spoke to Blanche; you may know her. She told me that he doesn't need one."

"Well, he does," he said.

"But I spoke to her on the phone. Blanche. You can call her. She assured me that we don't need one."

By now the line behind us was getting antsy as was the agent.

"Ma'am," he continued. "I don't care if the pope himself told you that your son doesn't need a passport. He cannot get on the plane to Mexico without one!"

By now Christian was in tears and Barry was dragging our suitcases out of line.

"What are we going to do?" I asked. It was clear that we were not getting on the plane that day.

In the end, we had to fly to Houston, one of the cities where you can get a same-day passport, stand in line for hours at the Federal Building, and the following day we boarded the plane for Mexico. Our vacation was salvaged.

One of the things that became clear to me is that in certain circumstances in our world, paperwork matters. If you've ever applied for a passport or a driver's license, applied for a student loan, bought a car or a home, you need to have your paperwork in order. Some paperwork is simply submitted; other paperwork needs to be responded to. If you failed to RSVP to a wedding invitation, for example, and you show up anyway, your name might not be on the guest list. You were not expected. An invitation expects a response.

Your Eternal Invitation Requires a Response

This will never be more eternally important than if you fail to respond to God's RSVP. Forgive me for using such a human term for such a life-defining moment. I don't mean to trivialize this in any way. It's far too important. The reality is that God has invited every man, woman, and child to spend eternity with him, but it's an invitation that requires a response. He sent this invitation out in the person of his Son, Jesus Christ, a flesh-and-blood invitation with an RSVP. It's a personal invitation, it's individual. It doesn't matter where you were born or what your family believes, God has personally invited you to be in relationship with him through trusting in his Son, Jesus. One of the best-known verses in Scripture is found in John's Gospel. It's regarded as the heart of God in a nutshell. I was eleven years old when I learned and responded to this verse in this translation:

For God so loved the world, that he gave his only begotten Son, that whosoever believeth in him should not perish, but have everlasting life. (John 3:16 KJV)

65

This is how it reads in the New Living Translation:

For this is how God loved the world: He gave his one and only Son, so that everyone who believes in him will not perish but have eternal life.

What an open invitation. It's sent out to "whosoever," to "everyone." I know what it feels like to be left out of something, not invited to something. I'm sure you do too. It doesn't feel good. It makes you question yourself. Did I do something wrong? Did I say something? School can be a harsh place to learn that we don't always fit in. I was not the cool kid. I was not the sporty kid. I eventually found my place with the music and drama students, but it was clear, especially at the school lunch tables, that there were places where I wasn't welcome.

> **When you recognize who Jesus is and respond to his invitation, you're welcomed in to stay forever.**

God is not like that. Whether you are eleven years old or ninety-two, rich or penniless, a model citizen or someone with a history of mistakes or bad choices, when you recognize who Jesus is and respond to his invitation, you're welcomed in to stay forever.

In chapter 2, we saw the eternal impact of that belief when we looked at the criminal who was executed beside Christ. He had a moment of recognition. He saw that Jesus was the Son of God, and in that moment of belief he cried out to him and was reassured that he would be with Jesus in paradise. He only had a few more hours to live. He didn't have time to clean up his act, read the Scriptures, attend a Bible study, or even attempt to right whatever wrongs landed him in prison in the first place. All he did was cry out to be saved and he was. Perhaps in heaven we'll hear the rest of his story, but what mattered in his last moments on earth was that his eyes were opened, he recognized and believed.

Jesus, I am a sinner. You are the Son of God. Save me!

But to all who believed him and accepted him, he gave the right to become children of God. (John 1:12)

Responding to God's invitation is the most important thing that any man, woman, or child can ever do. You can achieve incredible success in life or reach the peak of your profession, but if you don't know where you will spend eternity, you have missed the greatest invitation of all. The life Jesus offers is all about relationship, not about religion. There are many people who faithfully sit in church who have no personal relationship with Jesus. It's not about joining a club; it's about falling in love with a Savior—a love that will impact every area of your life.

For years I thought I understood what it meant to be in relationship with Jesus, but my understanding was based more on what I thought I needed to do rather than in what Christ had already done.

My Own Journey

Let me tell you a little about my own journey to understanding who Jesus is and what he did for us. My initial decision to follow him happened in a moment, but it took years for me to understand that what Jesus did was all that really mattered. It wasn't about what I could do. It was all about what he has done.

I was born into a Christian family in Scotland. By that I mean that my mum and dad were very involved in church, not just on a Sunday, but their belief in the person of Jesus impacted the daily decisions they made, how they raised us, how they viewed other people. We prayed together as a family. We read the Bible together. We were involved in the life of our village. Coal mining had been a big industry where we lived, but as the pits began to close and men lost their jobs, Dad would often invite families to join us for a meal where he would share his faith and pray for those who were struggling to survive. Life within the walls of our home was good; it made sense; it was safe.

All of that changed when I was five years old. My father's brain aneurysm impacted his ability to walk and talk, and it drastically altered his personality. My last encounter with my dad was a terrifying and violent one. After he was removed from our home and taken to a psychiatric hospital, he died by suicide.

We did all the same things we'd done before but with one less person around the dinner table. I didn't feel safe anymore. My mum didn't have the tools to know how to navigate her own terror and grief, never mind help three children who were under the age of seven. We still went to church and prayed together, but we never talked about what happened to our family. We never talked about where God is in the midst of suffering. Did he see? Did he care? We sang the same songs that talked about his faithfulness and goodness, but they didn't always make sense to me. God seemed detached and far away.

> **God has no grandchildren, only sons and daughters.**

That changed when I was eleven years old. I heard a Scottish evangelist talk about having a personal relationship with Jesus. That was news to me. I always thought that we admired God from a distance, knowing in some vague way he was looking down on us to see if we were behaving as we should. But the evangelist said that God wanted to know each one of us personally. He said that God has no grandchildren, only sons and daughters.

The implication was that just because your parents believed didn't mean you were included. It was not a package deal. Everyone got to choose for themselves. That evening, before I went to sleep, I asked my mum if she would pray with me so that I could become God's daughter. I remember feeling as though something inside me shifted. If I was now part of God's family, I wanted to live like it and tell other people about it. It felt like the most important thing I'd ever done, and I wanted to be good at it. I didn't want to mess it up.

One of the things I remember my mum telling me that evening would impact me for the next twenty-five years of my life. It would be good news to most people, but I heard it differently. She told me that as well as loving and following Jesus, I had a heavenly Father watching over me. That was wonderful and terrifying news. Wonderful because again I had a father. I had a father who loved me. Terrifying because a father's love could change in a moment. One moment arms would be open wide and the next there would be the back of a hand across my face. I decided that night that no matter how hard the Christian life was, I would be perfect. I remember thinking, "I've got this! I will not mess this up and lose the love of another father."

I Felt Too Broken

When trauma happens in childhood, it carves messages into our souls. Perhaps this is your story too. Whether it was physical, sexual, or verbal abuse, those broken places become the lens through which we view the world and the things we believe about ourselves.

I'm not good enough.

I'm too broken.

It was my fault.

There's something wrong with me.

The world's not safe.

Do what you're told.

Don't ask questions.

As the years went on, I became a very careful, obedient, fear-filled person. I wouldn't have dreamt of rebelling in any way. I made good decisions in life for all the wrong reasons. I'm glad now that I didn't throw myself into alcohol or drugs or sex, but it wasn't because I wanted to honor God. It was because I didn't want him to stop loving me. I've written more extensively about these years in previous books; suffice it to say here that just as life was interrupted at five and eleven, life as I knew it completely imploded at thirty-five. I had spent so many years trying to be good enough, trying to never fail, trying to never disappoint that I was beyond exhausted trying to be perfect. I felt weighed down by a lead coat of shame, or "not-enoughness." When I realized that with each passing day I was struggling to want to still be here, I reached out to a friend who is a psychologist and was admitted to a psychiatric hospital. It's one of the best things that ever happened to me, although it felt initially as if I'd gone to hell. I felt so alone. I was such a disappointment. What was crystal clear to me was that I was done. Whatever had worked for years no longer worked. I could not be good enough for God.

My Rebirth

When you are a patient in a psychiatric hospital, they take away things that you could hurt yourself with—hair dryer, belts, mirror, anything sharp. Ironically, they didn't take away the one thing that began to dismantle my wrong ideas about God, my Bible. I'd read my Bible before, voraciously, but always through a list-making lens.

What more could I do that would make God happy?
What should I avoid?
What does God expect?

Now I read it as a broken person. I read it with tears streaming down my face. I read it with the kind of desperate questions that

someone asks who has spent years in the church but was now cling-
ing by the fingernails onto the edge of life.

What is the point of my life?

Why am I here?

Why should I choose to go on living?

What is faith?

Why does it matter?

Why did Jesus come?

Why did he die?

Who did he die for?

What does he want from me?

I just wanted to go to heaven and be done with all the struggles.

No More Perfect Prayers

I found it hard to pray the way I was used to. I had no more perfect
prayers. Some days my prayers were tears. Some days just one word:
help! I finally stopped trying to impress God. I had nothing left. For
the four weeks I was a patient in the hospital, diagnosed with severe
clinical depression, I settled in the Gospel of John. I decided that
either every word was true, and if it was, it was everything I needed;
or it was all a lie and I could throw it away. When I had words, I
prayed very honest prayers.

God, if you are listening to me, please speak to me.

I read John's Gospel over and over, and I began to see Jesus with
fresh eyes. I saw the gift that he came to give, the love that he poured
out, and the beautiful picture that he painted of his Father. I'd known
John 3:16 since I was a child, but I began to understand it, not just
for the world but for me: "For this is how God loved the world: He

gave his one and only Son, so that everyone who believes in him will not perish but have eternal life."

The fact that God was willing to sacrifice his only Son and that Jesus was willing to come was overwhelming to me. He came, as I've heard someone say, "not to make bad people good but to make dead people live." That's how I felt. I felt dead inside, and I was tired of trying to be good. The news that God wanted me in heaven was mind-blowing. For all eternity God actually wants me there. That's God's invitation to you as well. He wants you to be with him for all eternity. You might have never felt included, not the "it" girl or the guy everyone else looks up to with the perfect golf handicap, but God wants you with him forever. When you look at yourself in the mirror you might see an expanding waistline or hair getting gray at the edges, or you might feel as if you never quite fit in, but God says, "I choose you. I love you."

> **I thought Christianity was all about doing. I finally realized it was all about done.**

The place of my greatest nightmares, a psychiatric hospital, became the place of my rebirth. I began to understand that it didn't matter where I worked or what I did, God's love for me would never change, would never be withdrawn. I was loved forever because of what Jesus had already done. I thought Christianity was all about *doing*. I finally realized it was all about *done*. It was already done!

> God saved you by his grace when you believed. And you can't take credit for this; it is a gift from God. Salvation is not a reward for the good things we have done, so none of us can boast about it. (Eph. 2:8–9)

It Is Finished!

There was one verse in particular in John's Gospel that reshaped how I understood everything that Jesus did. This took place when

Jesus was dying on the cross. He had been in agony for six hours, and then we read this:

> Jesus knew that his mission was now *finished*, and to fulfill Scripture he said, "I am thirsty." A jar of sour wine was sitting there, so they soaked a sponge in it, put it on a hyssop branch, and held it up to his lips. When Jesus had tasted it, he said, "*It is finished!*" Then he bowed his head and gave up his spirit. (John 19:28–30, emphasis added)

He finished his mission. He did everything he came to do. In the Greek, that phrase, "It is finished," is *tetelestai*. The above verses are the only two places in the New Testament where this word occurs. "The word *tetelestai* was also written on business documents or receipts in New Testament times . . . indicating that a bill had been paid in full."[1] When a bill is paid in full there is nothing more owed. It's paid. It's finished. It's done. Jesus came to pay the debt that we never could. His work was finished, and he fulfilled every prophecy in the Old Testament that spoke about what the coming Messiah would accomplish. He paid the price for my sin and for yours. We don't use the word *sin* very much anymore, but the bottom line is that God is perfect and holy and we're not. To make it possible for us to be in heaven forever, Jesus paid our bill, in full. It's impossible for us to understand the eternal implication of this fully. It's too great. Even the best human illustration falls short of what Christ did, although it can give us a little glimpse.

I read a deeply touching story online a few days ago that offers a human example of what it must feel like to have someone step in and pay a debt you can't possibly pay in the nick of time. It tells the story of the late Czar Nicholas of Russia, who used to wander around his barracks at night in disguise to get an accurate sense of what his soldiers were doing. One evening he saw a light on in a

> **When you place your trust in Jesus, your name is written in the Book of Life, and no one can remove it.**

room that should have been in darkness. When he opened the door, he saw the son of one of his old friends asleep at a table. Beside him was a loaded revolver, some money, and a sheet of paper. The story continues.

On the sheet of paper was a long list of debts, gambling, and other evil debts. The total ran into many thousands of rubles: the officer had used army funds to pay these wicked, reckless debts, and now, having worked till late into the night trying to get his accounts straight, had discovered for the first time how much he owed. It was hopeless, the pitifully small balance on hand left such a huge deficit to be made up! On the sheet of paper, below the terrible total, was written this question.–

"Who Can Pay So Great a Debt?"

Unable to face the disgrace, the officer had intended shooting himself, but completely worn out with sorrow and remorse, he had fallen asleep.

As the Czar realized what had happened, his first thought was to have the man immediately arrested, and in due course brought before a court martial. . . . But as he remembered the long friendship with the young officer's father, Love overcame Judgment, and in a moment he had devised a plan whereby he could be just towards the army and yet justify the culprit. The Czar took up the pen that had dropped from the hand of the wearied, hopeless offender and with his own hand answered the question with one word,–

"NICHOLAS"[2]

The following day, the Czar sent exactly what was owed. He paid the debt in full.

Love overcame judgment. That's what Jesus did for you and for me. Even though it would take years for me to begin to understand the depth of that love, on that winter's night on the west coast of

74

Scotland when I was eleven years old, something took place that changed my eternal destiny. When I said yes to loving and following Jesus, when I asked him to forgive me for my sin, my name was written in the Lamb's Book of Life.

> All who are victorious will be clothed in white. I will never erase their names from the Book of Life, but I will announce before my Father and his angels that they are mine. (Rev. 3:5)

When you place your trust in Jesus, your name is written in that book, and no one can remove it.

The Only Way to Heaven

One of the greatest gifts of my time in the hospital was finally understanding that God's love for me as a Father had nothing to do with what I get right or get wrong but is 100 percent based on what Christ finished. It's the same for you. I've heard people say that they think they'll go to heaven because they've lived a good life or they've been generous with their time and money, and I've heard people say that they feel lost and hopeless because they've made too many mistakes for God to forgive them. Neither of those things are true.

Whenever I start the whole process of preparing to write a book, I'll often jump on social media and ask a few questions just to get a feel for how the subject matter might sit with people, what questions they might want to ask in return. When I mentioned that I was going to write on the subject of heaven and wondered what people's thoughts about heaven were, there were some interesting comments.

"If God is a God of love, then we all go to heaven."
"I volunteer at a church, so I'm pretty sure I'm going to heaven."

"My parents were religious before they died. I'm sure they'll put in a good word for me."

There was another thread, however, that I found heartbreaking:

"I think I'm too broken for God."
"Have I messed up too badly?"
"I think it's too late for me."

The truth of the gospel is that no matter how hard we try to live good, honorable lives, we'll never live up to the standard of a holy God. The Bible makes it clear that we all fall short. "For everyone has sinned; we all fall short of God's glorious standard" (Rom. 3:23).

That's the hard truth about our lives. We try but it's not enough. The great news, however, for those who feel that they've messed up too badly is that no one is too broken or too far gone for the love of God to reach them. If you still have a pulse and there's not a white chalk mark around your body, it's not too late. The only question is, Have you responded to God's invitation?

The Invitation

In his final meal with his closest friends, Jesus made it very clear that life was about to become very confusing for them but everything that was going to happen was part of God's plan. He told them that he was going to prepare a place for them (as we looked at in chapter 1), but then he continued on.

"And you know the way to where I am going."
"No, we don't know, Lord," Thomas said. "We have no idea where you are going, so how can we know the way?"
Jesus told him, "I am the way, the truth, and the life. No one can come to the Father except through me." (John 14:4–6)

Even though they had been with Jesus for three years, there was so much that was still a mystery to them. They watched him perform miracles, feed thousands with a young boy's lunch, and raise the dead, but their greatest expectation of the promised Messiah was that he would free his people from those who were ruling over them and set up his kingdom here on earth. The Jewish people had lived under Roman rule for so long, and they wanted to be free. They didn't understand that Jesus had come to change the whole world for every one of us—Jews and gentiles. He told them that night, "You know the way to where I am going." I understand Thomas's confusion when he replied, "We've no idea where you are going." It must have seemed as if Jesus was talking in riddles. Then he made one of the most important, clarifying statements ever given:

I am the way, the truth, and the life. No one can come to the Father except through me. (John 14:6)

There is nothing about this statement that is ambiguous or confusing. Jesus made it as simple and clear as possible. "I am the way." There are not a million different ways to heaven or a thousand different doors. Heaven is not the default destination for every human being; we get to choose. We are invited to respond to God's invitation to life. We can't even begin to imagine how mind-blowing heaven will be. I want you to be there. Way more importantly, God wants you to be there. That's why Jesus came. When Paul wrote to the church in Rome, he made the invitation very clear: "If you openly declare that Jesus is Lord and believe in your heart that God raised him from the dead, you will be saved" (Rom. 10:9).

So to the question, "Does everyone go to heaven?" the answer is simple. Every single person who responds to God's invitation through Christ will spend eternity with Jesus. Those who don't, will not. It has become very politically incorrect to speak about the reality of hell, but hell is a real place. In the end, it is total separation from

God forever. Of all the doctrines of the faith that I have wrestled with in life there is none more troubling to me than that of hell, and yet Scripture makes it very clear: "And anyone whose name was not found recorded in the Book of Life was thrown into the lake of fire" (Rev. 20:15).

Jesus talked about the reality of hell, not to scare those who listened to him but to call us to come to him for help and hope and forgiveness. "Don't be afraid of those who want to kill your body; they cannot touch your soul. Fear only God, who can destroy both soul and body in hell" (Matt. 10:28).

God's invitation is still open. It's not too late to RSVP.

As a Scot, I love this true story about a Scottish minister, John Harper, who had been invited to preach at Moody Bible Church in Chicago. He had no idea when he boarded the ship that he would not survive the trip or ever return to Scotland, but when you know without a shadow of a doubt where you will spend eternity, it changes how you live on earth, even if you only have a few moments left.

And so it was that John Harper, his sister, and his six-year-old daughter (his wife had died) found themselves on the great ship, the *Titanic*. Survivors later reported that as *Titanic* began to sink, Harper admonished people to be prepared to die. He made sure his sister and daughter were in a lifeboat even as he continued to share the Gospel with whoever would listen. And when he found himself in the icy water with a life jacket, floating near another man, Harper asked, "Are you saved?"

"No, I'm not saved!" the desperate man replied.

"Believe on the Lord Jesus Christ and you will be saved!" Harper shouted.

One report says Harper, knowing he could not survive long in the icy water, took off his life jacket and threw it to another person with the words, "You need this more than I do!" Moments later, Harper disappeared beneath the water. Four years later, when there was a reunion of the survivors of the *Titanic,* the man to whom Harper had witnessed told the story of his rescue and gave a testimony of his conversion recorded in a tract, *I was John Harper's Last Convert.*[3]

That's a life well lived. When you know that you are loved so extravagantly and promised life eternally, it's hard to keep it to yourself.

Father God,
Thank you that I can know without a shadow of a doubt
that I will spend eternity in heaven through faith in your Son,
Jesus. Jesus, thank you for paying a debt that I could never pay.
Amen.

What I Know about Heaven

By placing my faith in Jesus, I am guaranteed a place in heaven.

5

MY DOG, MY CAT, AND WILL I BE FAT?

If they had longed for the country they came from, they could have gone back. But they were looking for a better place, a heavenly homeland. That is why God is not ashamed to be called their God, for he has prepared a city for them.

Hebrews 11:15–16

I t started with an innocent pink ticket. Barry, Christian, and I were waiting in line at an amusement park to see an animal show. As it was the last show of the day and the theater only held a hundred people, the attendant was handing out the appropriate number of pink tickets so no one would wait in line only to discover the theater was full. When he got to us, he had only two tickets left. I told Barry to take Christian in and I'd wait, but he insisted that I go in with Christian and he'd wait for us. Christian and I hurried in and took our seats, but the whole *needing a ticket to get in* thing was clearly on his mind. He asked if he could have his ticket to hold and then

I noticed that he folded it carefully and put it in the pocket of his jeans. When we got home that evening and Christian was bathed, exhausted, and in bed, I saw that he had unfolded the ticket and it was on his nightstand. I picked it up to throw it away, but he asked me to leave it where it was. He had a plan for it.

The following day when I was shaking out our dog Belle's bed, the pink ticket fell out. I had no idea why it was there. At supper I mentioned it to Christian and asked if he knew that his pink ticket was in Belle's basket.

"Yes, Mom, I do," he said. "I put it there. It's so she can get in."

"I'm not sure Belle wants to go to the amusement park," I said.

"It's not for the park," he said. "It's so she can get into heaven. It's her pink ticket."

I explained to him that we don't need a ticket to get into heaven, that it's because we trust in Jesus. He looked a little exasperated as he told me that, yes, he knew that, but the Bible didn't specifically say what your dog might need.

"Belle won't be able to say anything to Jesus, Mom, but if she has a pink ticket, she should be good."

And so "pink ticket salvation for animals" was born in our home. (Yes, I am aware that this is not theologically sound.) When we added Tink, a French bichon, to our crew, the ticket was halved. When Maggie the Yorkie made her debut, the two halves were glued together, then cut into thirds. As the years have passed, we've laughed as a family at Christian's childlike commitment to ensuring his dogs' future. Having said that, I do realize that people have a lot of similar, practical questions about heaven. "Will my dog be there?" is right up there with the rest of them. So I decided in this chapter I'd answer a few of the most common questions about heaven. Some answers we know for sure, based on what is specifically addressed in the Bible. Others are conclusions we can reasonably come to, based on other biblical information and the character of God. So let's just start with animals.

Will There Be Animals in Heaven?

Our five-year-old son had requested a family meeting. As there are only three of us, it was fairly easy to assemble quickly. Before he began, he asked us to let him finish what he had to say before we asked any questions. We agreed. It was quite an impassioned speech about companionship and friends and talking and listening. His concluding line was, "So, as you can see, I *need* a dog." He rested his case.

Being freed up apparently to now comment, I said, "I've heard of lots of people wanting a dog, babe. Not necessarily *needing* a dog unless it was a service dog."

"I need someone to talk to," Christian explained.

"You can talk to us," Barry answered.

"I mean *about you*," he clarified.

Excellent point. We bought Belle that weekend.

It is hard to put into words the love that pets bring to us as humans. I'm constantly moved by pictures on social media of the strong bond that exists between pets and their owners, and pets and each other. In fact, if you checked out who I follow on Instagram, over half of them are animals. They bring so much joy. Animals have always been part of our story. When we go right back to the beginning at creation, before God created Eve from one of Adam's ribs, he populated Eden with all sorts of wonderful creatures.

It was God's original plan that we would live together with the animals in peace and harmony. It's not unreasonable to think that if that was God's original plan in Eden, then someday we will once again enjoy these beautiful gifts from God.

In the revelation given to John, he heard Jesus say from the throne, "Look, I am making everything new!" (Rev. 21:5).

Jesus doesn't say I'm making *new things*. He says I'm making *everything new*. That has to include everything God created in Eden, the perfect garden where Adam was asked to give a name to every creature.

Reading in Genesis 6, we see once again the importance of animals to God's creation. When God determined to flood the earth because of the excessive wickedness, his instructions to Noah as he built his boat were to make sure that the animals survived as well.

> Bring a pair of every kind of animal—a male and a female—into the boat with you to keep them alive during the flood. Pairs of every kind of bird, and every kind of animal, and every kind of small animal that scurries along the ground, will come to you to be kept alive. And be sure to take on board enough food for your family and for all the animals. (Gen. 6:19–21)

So what do we know for sure about animals in heaven? Well, we certainly know that there are horses in heaven. As we saw in chapter 2, Elijah was taken up to heaven in a carriage of fire drawn by horses (2 Kings 2:11). In Revelation 6 we read, "I looked up and saw a white horse standing there. Its rider carried a bow, and a crown was placed on his head. He rode out to win many battles and gain the victory" (v. 2).

If animals were always part of God's plan for us, I'm sure they will be part of our eternal lives with him. In heaven we will be who we are now, but without sin, so animals that knew a certain beauty, grace, and strength in Eden will be perfected once again too. (Perhaps our dog Maggie will stop barking?)

Isaiah the prophet wrote about our future home.

> In that day the wolf and the lamb will live together;
>   the leopard will lie down with the baby goat.
> The calf and the yearling will be safe with the lion,
>   and a little child will lead them all.
> The cow will graze near the bear.
>   The cub and the calf will lie down together.
> The lion will eat hay like a cow.

> The baby will play safely near the hole of a cobra.
>> Yes, a little child will put its hand in a nest of deadly snakes without harm.
> Nothing will hurt or destroy in all my holy mountain,
>> for as the waters fill the sea,
>> so the earth will be filled with people who know the Lord.
>> (11:6–9)

The question may remain, however, "What about my pet? Will my dog be there or just newly created dogs and cats?" I love what my friend Joni Eareckson Tada shared in one of her books as she thought about heaven.

> If God brings our pets back to life, it wouldn't surprise me. It would be just like Him. It would be totally in keeping with His generous character . . . Exorbitant. Excessive. Extravagant in grace after grace. Of all the dazzling discoveries and ecstatic pleasures heaven will hold for us, the potential of seeing Scrappy would be pure whimsy—utterly, joyfully, surprisingly superfluous.[1]

Billy Graham was once asked by a young girl if her dog would be in heaven. He asked her if that would make her happy. When she assured him that it would, he said he was sure her dog would be there.[2]

Have you ever wished that your dog or cat could talk? I know I have. I think it's fascinating that when the serpent talked to Eve in the garden of Eden, she wasn't surprised that he could talk.

> The serpent was the shrewdest of all the wild animals the LORD God had made. One day he asked the woman, "Did God really say you must not eat the fruit from any of the trees in the garden?" (Gen. 3:1)

Wouldn't it be wonderful if in heaven all the animals have the ability to talk? We can't know that now, but I'm sure that as we will

85

live pure lives free of sin, mistrust, and fear, animals will be raised to the existence and nobility they knew in Eden before the fall.

Will I Be Fat in Heaven?

Before I came to live in America, I worked with Youth for Christ in England as a youth evangelist and singer. Most of my work entailed going into high schools and teaching religious education classes and speaking at assemblies. We would host after-school clubs and evening events. One of my favorite people to work with was a wild and crazy Greek youth evangelist, J. John. He is one of the funniest people I've ever met, and he is a brilliant communicator. Speaking to high school students who would rather be anywhere but in religious education class is not a job for the faint of heart, but he was so gifted in capturing their attention and explaining the gospel in ways they could relate to. He has written many books over the years, but when I received his latest one in the mail it made me laugh. It's simply called *Will I Be Fat in Heaven? and Other Curious Questions.*

When you pause and think about that for a moment, it's actually a fabulous question. Not so much the idea of being fat or thin but what will we look like, what age will we be, will we be able to eat anything we want without consequences? I've often joked to friends that I'm only going to eat carbs for the first thousand years in heaven to make up for any I've sacrificed here on earth; my assumption being that no matter what we eat there we won't gain weight. Clearly, I'm operating on a shaky human perspective. But what will our bodies be like? This is what my friend J. John suggests, and I agree.

Our new bodies will be perfect and glorious. Now although that's an idea that greatly appeals to me when I look in the mirror, step on the scales or go to the doctor, neither I, nor anybody else, knows exactly what that means. Nevertheless, what we will have will be a definite improvement on the disintegrating bodies we have now. Those of us who follow Christ are not going to merely get some cosmetic makeover, but a whole-body upgrade! . . . Because heaven is a place of perfection, I think we will each have a perfect body in shape and size. We definitely won't be visiting Weight Watchers! We will be whole and healthy, no pains, aches, no diseases and with 20:20 vision as there will be so much to see. Will I be fat in heaven? No! I will be happy and content with everything.[3]

All the things that bother us about our bodies here on earth will be gone forever. We won't give anything like that a second thought. Are you a people watcher? It's one of my favorite things to do when I'm in an airport. My latest flight was running two hours behind schedule, so knowing that I was going home to work on this chapter, I decided to pay extra attention to everyone around me. There was quite a slice of life hurrying through the terminal. The following are simply observations, not judgments.

A harassed-looking mom trying to corral three children who must have all been under five, one of whom was having a total meltdown.

An elderly man being pushed in a wheelchair. He was wearing a hat commemorating his years of service in the military. He was missing his right leg below the knee.

A significantly overweight young girl carrying a box of doughnuts.

A businessman staring at his reflection in the window, trying to cover his balding spot.

Let me throw myself in too. I'm slightly limping. I'm not sure yet what's wrong with my right knee, but it clicks when I walk and sometimes it's really painful. I'm tired and I obviously didn't manage to take all my eye makeup off last night as I look a bit like a startled badger.

I felt such a wave of compassion and love flood over me as I looked at us all, hurrying through life, doing the best we can most days and yet falling into bed every night exhausted before a new one begins.

So, for those of us who love Jesus and have trusted him with our eternal lives, let's unpack some of the most frequently asked questions about heaven.

What Will We Look Like in Heaven?

Someone asked the apostle Paul that question, and apparently, he thought it was a bit of a stupid question. This is what he had to say:

> But someone may ask, "How will the dead be raised? What kind of bodies will they have?" What a foolish question! When you put a seed into the ground, it doesn't grow into a plant unless it dies first. And what you put in the ground is not the plant that will grow, but only a bare seed of wheat or whatever you are planting. Then God gives it the new body he wants it to have. A different plant grows from each kind of seed. Similarly, there are different kinds of flesh—one kind for humans, another for animals, another for birds, and another for fish.
>
> There are also bodies in the heavens and bodies on the earth. The glory of the heavenly bodies is different from the glory of the earthly bodies. The sun has one kind of glory, while the moon and stars each have another kind. And even the stars differ from each other in their glory.
>
> It is the same way with the resurrection of the dead. Our earthly bodies are planted in the ground when we die, but they will be raised to live forever. Our bodies are buried in brokenness, but they will be raised in glory. They are buried in weakness, but they will be raised in strength. (1 Cor. 15:35–43)

Once we get over Paul's initial exasperation with the question, there are great things to glean from this. I don't know if you are much of a gardener. I am not, but my grandmother was. I would watch her take little brown seeds or bulbs that looked like nothing at all, and she would plant them in her flower beds. I was always amazed at what came up each spring, beautiful flowers in glorious colors. I think Paul is trying to help us see that when we look at the lives we live right now, it's impossible to see the beauty that will be when we are reborn in heaven. We are buried in brokenness and raised in glory. Buried in weakness but raised in strength. Our present bodies have a limited shelf life, but our new bodies will have no expiration date. They will never let us down.

As I get older, I get frustrated that things I used to be able to do without thinking about them now need careful consideration. I have always been a huge roller-coaster fan, the bigger, the badder, the better. Now I have to think about my neck and my back surgery. Our heavenly bodies will be better than we have ever been. We'll never get tired or worn out. I don't know if there will be roller coasters in heaven or not, but if there are, I'll see you in line!

Will Shame and Pain Be Gone Forever?

One thing I know for absolute sure is that all fear, shame, and pain will be gone forever. There will be no more cancer or heart problems, no anxiety or depression or panic attacks. No loneliness or self-doubt. No more aching joints and aching backs. No more children dying and marriages falling apart. No more broken bones and broken hearts. All of that will be gone forever. Can you imagine what that will be like? It's hard to grasp.

I was diagnosed many years ago with clinical depression, and over the years I've learned how to manage it pretty well. I'm faithful in taking my medication, and I try to get some exercise and eat well most of the time, but I still live with its shadow over many of my days. That heaviness will be gone forever. I have friends who deal with panic attacks. They have told me that it feels as if they are dying until they are able to control their breathing and take a few moments to return to a place that feels safe. Mental illness is a heavy weight to carry. If you or a loved one deal with that, my heart is with you. It may be an invisible struggle, but it is a potent one. I pray that you have the courage to take care of yourself and to get the help you need. If you take medication, don't allow anyone to shame you or make you feel as if somehow your love for Christ is less. When I have tried over the years to come off my medication, that's when very dark thoughts overwhelm me. I carried shame for so many years. The way it felt to me was that somehow, at some core level, not that I had *done* something wrong but that I *was* something wrong. During my psych ward stay I found great freedom meditating on Psalm 34. David wrote it at one of the lowest points in his life and yet he said, "Those who look to him for help will be radiant with joy; no shadow of shame will darken their faces" (v. 5).

There is still a lot of ignorance in the church about the reality of mental illness. I was speaking at a church on the East Coast and mentioned that my father died by suicide and how much I was looking forward to seeing him again in heaven. At the end of my message, a teenage girl asked if she could talk to me. Through her wracking sobs she told me that her dad, who had been a wonderful father and a very active member of their church but had struggled with severe depression for most of his life, had died by suicide. She had been told by other church members that her father was now in hell. How cruel. How wrong. There is only one unforgivable sin and that is rejecting the Son of God.

> "When you stand before God, you won't be judged by the last thing you did before you died but by the last thing Jesus did before he died."

I read a powerful article by Randy Alcorn titled "Suicide, Heaven, and Jesus—the Final Answer to Our Sorrow." I highly recommend it as a helpful resource. In it he talks about the suicide of a young associate pastor in California and references statements made by Greg Laurie, the senior pastor who conducted his memorial service. Greg reminded those who were grief-stricken, "When you stand before God, you won't be judged by the last thing you did before you died but by the last thing Jesus did before he died."[4]

Christ paid for all of our sin, and Paul reminds us so powerfully at the conclusion of Romans 8:

And I am convinced that nothing can ever separate us from God's love. Neither death nor life, neither angels nor demons, neither our fears for today nor our worries about tomorrow—not even the powers of hell can separate us from God's love. No power in the sky above or in the earth below—indeed, nothing in all creation will ever be able to separate us from the love of God that is revealed in Christ Jesus our Lord. (vv. 38–39)

On one of my visits to stay with Ruth Bell Graham, I remember we sat in her garden in Montreat, North Carolina, on a sunny afternoon sipping tea. Ruth knew that my father had died by suicide and she said to me, "When a believer takes their own life, God hasn't called them home but he welcomes them home."

I believe that is true. If you do struggle with those kinds of thoughts, may I remind you again that the devil is a liar. He would love to make you believe that your life doesn't matter, that no one would miss you if you were gone. Don't believe him. Your life matters. Get help. Reach out to someone. If you have no one to talk to right now where you are, you can call 988 and talk to someone.

Run that race. Finish that fight, and remember, whatever you have struggled with in your life, big or small, will be gone forever when you are finally home with Jesus. Let me say that again.

Your life matters!

Run that race!

Finish that fight!

How Old Will We Be in Heaven?

My dad died when he was thirty-four. My mum was eighty-six. So how old will they be in heaven? Will they be the ages they were when they died? Scripture doesn't address this directly, but there are certain things that can guide our thinking. Adam and Eve were not born as children. They were created presumably in the prime of life. They were never supposed to age because aging was a result of sin. Christ died when he was approximately thirty-three (Luke 3:23 tells us that he was about thirty years old when he began his public ministry, and he was in ministry for three years). Many theologians agree that in heaven we will be at the age that would have been prime in life, which could be in our late twenties or early thirties. In the thirteenth century, Italian theologian Thomas Aquinas wrote,

> All will rise in the condition of perfect age, which is of thirty-two or thirty-three years. This is because all who were not yet arrived at this age, did not possess this perfect age, and the old had already lost it. Hence, youths and children will be given what they lack, and what the aged once had will be restored to them.[5]

That's an interesting and lovely thought, but as he didn't provide any specific Scripture to support this theory, it remains as such—a theory. What we do know is that we will be more alive than we have ever been, ready to serve, ready to love, ready to worship. There will be no more need for our spiritual armor because the battle will be over. I love how J. C. Ryle, a favorite scholar of mine, describes our home:

> Heaven shall be a place of perfect rest and peace. They who dwell there have no more conflict with the world, the flesh, and the devil; their warfare is finished, and their fight is fought; at length they may lay aside the armor of God; at last they may say to the sword of the Spirit—"rest and be still." They watch no longer, for they have no spiritual enemies to fear.[6]

No more warfare, no more need for spiritual armor.

> Surely your goodness and unfailing love will pursue me
>> all the days of my life,
> and I will live in the house of the LORD forever. (Ps. 23:6)

Will My Baby Be in Heaven?

As I've touched on in a previous chapter, one of the most heartbreaking things in life is to lose a child. To have held and nursed a little one, to have looked into those precious eyes and then to lose them must be an unbearable pain. I spent some time with a mother who was deeply distressed not only because of the devastating loss of her child but by what she had been told by a member of her church who had quoted part of Psalm 51 to her: "For I was born a sinner—yes, from the moment my mother conceived me" (v. 5).

As her little one had been too young to ask for forgiveness, this man suggested to her that her child might be eternally lost. I was horrified by the cruelty of this man and his lack of understanding of the heart of God. In his interactions with little children Jesus made it clear that children have a special place in his kingdom.

> About that time the disciples came to Jesus and asked, "Who is greatest in the Kingdom of Heaven?"
>
> Jesus called a little child to him and put the child among them. Then he said, "I tell you the truth, unless you turn from your sins and become like little children, you will never get into the Kingdom of Heaven. So anyone who becomes as humble as this little child is the greatest in the Kingdom of Heaven." (Matt. 18:1–4)

I don't have a shadow of a doubt that children who die are immediately carried into the presence of the Lord where they are safe and loved and free, waiting for the day when they will be reunited with their families. So too with little ones lost through miscarriage or abortion. I got pregnant one more time after our son was born but was only able to carry that child for a few weeks. I can't wait to be reunited in heaven. I think the baby was a girl.

Will There Be Angels in Heaven?

When I was a little girl, my favorite hobby was collecting what we called scraps. I don't know if these were ever popular in America, but I loved them and had a huge collection. Scraps are small paper images printed lithographically in all sorts of shapes and sizes. When I was in primary school in Scotland (elementary school in the US), we would take our scraps to school and swap them. Out of curiosity, I just googled "scraps collection" to see what would come up and was blown away. The very scraps I collected as a child are still available, and looking at the angel ones I used to collect made me smile. They are still available just as I remembered them. Half of the angels are blonde with bright red lipstick. The others are chubby with curly hair, perched on fluffy clouds leaning on their elbows presumably thinking deep thoughts.

These images are far removed from the angels we read about in Scripture. The first thing we know about them is that they must be fairly terrifying to look at as every time they make an appearance they say, "Don't be afraid!"

> Suddenly, an angel of the Lord appeared among them, and the radiance of the Lord's glory surrounded them. They were terrified, but the angel reassured them. "Don't be afraid!" (Luke 2:9–10)

I think we will be awestruck when we first see the angels. Even Daniel, who if you remember had survived a night in a den of lions, wasn't prepared for the sight.

> On April 23, as I was standing on the bank of the great Tigris River, I looked up and saw a man dressed in linen clothing, with a belt of

pure gold around his waist. His body looked like a precious gem. His face flashed like lightning, and his eyes flamed like torches. His arms and feet shone like polished bronze, and his voice roared like a vast multitude of people.

Only I, Daniel, saw this vision. The men with me saw nothing, but they were suddenly terrified and ran away to hide. So I was left there all alone to see this amazing vision. My strength left me, my face grew deathly pale, and I felt very weak. Then I heard the man speak, and when I heard the sound of his voice, I fainted and lay there with my face to the ground. (Dan. 10:4–9)

We are ill-prepared for the wonders we will see. Angels have many roles in our lives. One of the loveliest is the account we're given in Luke 16. Jesus told a story of two men who died: one, a very rich man, and the other, Lazarus, a beggar. When Lazarus died it was angels who carried him to heaven.

Jesus said, "There was a certain rich man who was splendidly clothed in purple and fine linen and who lived each day in luxury. At his gate lay a poor man named Lazarus who was covered with sores. As Lazarus lay there longing for scraps from the rich man's table, the dogs would come and lick his open sores. Finally, the poor man died and was carried by the angels to sit beside Abraham at the heavenly banquet." (vv. 19–22)

In those days, a poor man who died owning nothing wouldn't even be given a decent burial. His body would be tossed into the smoldering town dump of Gehenna, southwest of Jerusalem. Lazarus's body might have had no value on earth, but because of his faith he was carried by the angels into his eternal reward. God sent his heavenly escorts to bring his child home.

Angels are also called "ministering spirits." They physically strengthened Jesus after he had fasted for forty days in the wilderness and on the night when he was betrayed. He was emotionally and physically wrung out as he wept in Gethsemane. Luke, the doctor, tells us in his Gospel that Jesus was in such agony of soul that he literally sweat blood. We read, "Then an angel from heaven appeared and strengthened him. He prayed more fervently, and he was in such agony of spirit that his sweat fell to the ground like great drops of blood" (22:43–44).

Angels also protect and deliver. Acts 12 begins with the sad story of the execution of the apostle James. We read that King Herod Agrippa had begun to track down the apostles and have them killed.

> About that time King Herod Agrippa began to persecute some believers in the church. He had the apostle James (John's brother) killed with a sword. When Herod saw how much this pleased the Jewish people, he also arrested Peter. (This took place during the Passover celebration.) Then he imprisoned him, placing him under the guard of four squads of four soldiers each. (vv. 1–4)

After having James beheaded (the angels would have carried James right into Jesus's presence), Herod intended to put Peter on trial and have him executed too, but God had other plans. Herod had him guarded by sixteen guards. Imagine this scene. Peter is fast asleep. He's chained between two guards, with more at his cell door and another two sets of four posted further down the corridor, when suddenly an angel appears and tells him to get up and follow him.

> Then the angel told him, "Get dressed and put on your sandals." And he did. "Now put on your coat and follow me," the angel ordered.
> So Peter left the cell, following the angel. But all the time he thought it was a vision. He didn't realize it was actually happening. They passed the first and second guard posts and came to the iron gate leading to the city, and this opened for them all by itself. So they passed through and started walking down the street, and then the angel suddenly left him. (vv. 8–10)

Very practical angel—get dressed and put on your sandals!

God is a God of miracles. I'm telling you; we haven't seen anything yet. The amazing thing is that no matter how magnificent and powerful the angels are, they all bow down to Jesus. We might be startled by the sight of angels, but we will be forever captivated by the sight of Jesus, the only One who is worthy of our worship.

> **We will be forever captivated by the sight of Jesus, the only one who is worthy of our worship.**

How many angels do you think there are in heaven? Scripture makes it clear that there are millions upon millions. After John is given the revelation of heaven, he tries to describe what he saw with words he knows.

> Then I looked again, and I heard the voices of thousands and millions of angels around the throne and of the living beings and the elders. And they sang in a mighty chorus:
>
> "Worthy is the Lamb who was slaughtered—
>   to receive power and riches
> and wisdom and strength
>   and honor and glory and blessing."
>
> And then I heard every creature in heaven and on earth and under the earth and in the sea. They sang:
>
> "Blessing and honor and glory and power
>   belong to the one sitting on the throne
>   and to the Lamb forever and ever." (Rev. 5:11–13)

Think of the best worship event that you have ever been part of, and it doesn't come close. I remember being at an event with twenty-two thousand women singing as one voice. I had to stop singing because it was so beautiful. I had tears running down my face. That wasn't even a foretaste of what worship will be like in heaven.

What Will Worship Be Like in Heaven?

If you'd like to catch a glimpse of what worship will look like in heaven, read Revelation 4 and 5. Several of the commentaries I use describe them as the most complete picture of how glorious heavenly worship is, and we get a sneak peek. This is how the apostle John sets up where he was and what he was about to share.

> I, John, am your brother and your partner in suffering and in God's Kingdom and in the patient endurance to which Jesus calls us. I was exiled to the island of Patmos for preaching the word of God and for my testimony about Jesus. (Rev. 1:9)

When John was given his first glimpse of Jesus in all his resurrected, heavenly glory, he fell at his feet.

> When I saw him, I fell at his feet as if I were dead. But he laid his right hand on me and said, "Don't be afraid! I am the First and the Last. I am the living one. I died, but look—I am alive forever and ever! And I hold the keys of death and the grave." (vv. 17–18)

Then John was given an unimaginable gift—an open door and an invitation.

> Then as I looked, I saw a door standing open in heaven, and the same voice I had heard before spoke to me like a trumpet blast. The voice said, "Come up here, and I will show you what must happen after this." And instantly I was in the Spirit, and I saw a throne in heaven and someone sitting on it. The one sitting on the throne was as brilliant as gemstones—like jasper and carnelian. And the glow of an emerald circled his throne like a rainbow. Twenty-four thrones surrounded him, and twenty-four elders sat on them. They were all clothed in white and had gold crowns on their heads. From the throne came flashes of lightning and the rumble of thunder. And in front of the throne were seven torches with burning flames. This is

the sevenfold Spirit of God. In front of the throne was a shiny sea of glass, sparkling like crystal.

In the center and around the throne were four living beings, each covered with eyes, front and back. The first of these living beings was like a lion; the second was like an ox; the third had a human face; and the fourth was like an eagle in flight. Each of these living beings had six wings, and their wings were covered all over with eyes, inside and out. Day after day and night after night they keep on saying,

"Holy, holy, holy is the Lord God, the Almighty—
the one who always was, who is, and who is still to come."

Whenever the living beings give glory and honor and thanks to the one sitting on the throne (the one who lives forever and ever), the twenty-four elders fall down and worship the one sitting on the throne (the one who lives forever and ever). And they lay their crowns before the throne and say,

"You are worthy, O Lord our God,
to receive glory and honor and power.
For you created all things,
and they exist because you created what you pleased."
(4:1–11)

It's beyond our imagination, and yet one day it will be our home. I love how Jesus defined worship to a Samaritan woman. She wanted to know if the Jews had chosen the right place to worship or if the Samaritans had. This is what Jesus said: "But the time is coming—indeed it's here now—when true worshipers will worship the Father in spirit and in truth" (John 4:23).

The word *truth* in the original Greek is *aletheia*, which means "with nothing hidden," pure and transparent. That's how Jesus described true worship, with nothing hidden. I think one of the most amazing things about worship in heaven is that we will no longer be distracted by anything or anyone else. Our focus will all be on Jesus. How many times in a worship service have you noticed what someone on the platform is wearing or if the guitarist has had a haircut? Billy Graham wrote that in some circles we have come "dangerously close to worshipping our worship."[7] In heaven that will be no more. When we see Jesus in all his glory, we will have eyes for him and only him.

Can I Lose My Salvation?

There are so many things in life, great and small, that are uncertain.

Will my flight be on time?
Will I lose my job in tough times?
Will I be able to pay all my bills this month?
Will my child get into college?

The list is endless, but I want you to know one thing for sure. When you have given your life over to Jesus, when you have asked him to forgive you for the wrongs you have done in your life and you believe that he is the Son of God and that he died and rose again, you can know without a shadow of a doubt that you are saved, you are loved, and you are free. No one can snatch you from the Father's hand.

> **No one can snatch you from the Father's hand.**

My sheep listen to my voice; I know them, and they follow me. I give them eternal life, and they will never perish. No one can snatch them away from me, for my Father has given them to me, and he is more powerful than anyone else. No one can snatch them from the Father's hand. (John 10:27–29)

When We Finally See Jesus

There are so many glorious truths about heaven, but the greatest is that we will finally be with Jesus. We will see him not as a fragile baby or a man with the dust of the Galilean roads on his feet, and not as the bruised and bloodied One who was nailed to a tree and then laid in a borrowed tomb. We will see him as he is in all his glory, breathtakingly beautiful, and we will join our voices with the millions upon millions of angels and our brothers and sisters calling out, "Worthy is the Lamb, who was slain, to receive power and wealth and wisdom and strength and honor and glory and praise!" (Rev. 5:12 NIV).

I used to think that I would want answers to so many questions when I get to heaven, but I think now that seeing him will be all the answer I need.

Father God,

I can only imagine what it will be like to finally be home and be able to worship you in all your glory. This side of heaven I have many questions, but I know when I see Jesus face-to-face, all my questions will be gone.

Amen.

What I Know about Heaven

When I get home, I know that I will see and recognize my loved ones. All pain and shame will be gone, and I will join my voice with all my brothers and sisters through the ages and the millions upon millions of angels and worship Jesus as I've never done before.

6

IS HEAVEN WHAT I'VE BEEN LONGING FOR ALL ALONG?

How lovely is your dwelling place,
O Lord of Heaven's Armies.
I long, yes, I faint with longing
to enter the courts of the Lord.

Psalm 84:1–2

Barry and Christian were beyond excited. We were finally going to a football game at the new AT&T stadium to see our team, the Dallas Cowboys, play. The old stadium was great but nothing like we'd been promised with this brand-new one. It was state-of-the-art everything. It had a retractable roof and the largest screens ever for a football stadium. Christian had done his homework and was ready with all the statistics. He read the following off his phone as we sat in the massive line of fans in cars waiting to get in and see this wonder of wonders.

"Okay guys, listen to this. It has two high-definition screens, seventy-two feet by one hundred and sixty feet, that can display an almost life-size game to fans sitting anywhere in the stadium. It's so amazing it will make any seat a front row seat. With a total surface area of over twenty-five thousand square feet, the video board weighs a shocking 1.2 million pounds, the equivalent of roughly eighteen and a half fire trucks. Wow! And the hot dogs are huge."

When we finally made it to our seats I have to say, it was impressive. The only strange thing was that the screens were so big I ended up watching the screens rather than the game that was being played on the field. So it was kind of like I was watching it at home on television but with ninety thousand of my closest friends.

I am an ardent football fan. What we call football in Scotland, where I grew up, is soccer here in America. American football is something quite different. At first, the rules of the game made no sense to me. I couldn't believe they were allowed to pick up the ball and run with it.

I'd never been to a live game before. I was on my feet for most of the time. The only thing I found confusing were the signs that various people held up when the opposing team's offense took the field.

"Why are they holding up those signs?" I asked Barry.

"To encourage our team to bring it!" he said.

"Why would bringing gates help them?" I asked, genuinely confused.

"What do you mean?" he said.

"They're holding up signs saying, D, with a picture of a gate. How will that help?"

"That would be a fence," he said. "As in D-FENCE."

Looked like a gate to me.

I've lived and learned and am now a dyed-in-the-wool, win-or-lose Dallas Cowboys fan. Every season I wonder if this will be the one where we go all the way to the Super Bowl. I long to see that; I keep hoping, but thus far it's an unfulfilled longing.

Longing for Heaven

Do we long for heaven as much as we long for things on this earth? If not, why not? When it comes to the idea of longing for heaven, I wonder if we struggle with that because of what we have experienced here on earth.

The apostle Paul genuinely longed for heaven. What happened in Paul's life that impacted him in such a way that he longed to be in heaven? I believe it was because of the gift of what he experienced here on earth: two life-changing events.

I think Paul had quite an advantage over us in terms of how he not only physically experienced the risen Christ but also actually visited heaven. I believe these gifts were given to him because of all he was going to suffer as a follower of Jesus. If you remember, he had a very dramatic conversion. Paul was an educated, committed Jew who had no time for this new group of people who called themselves followers of Christ, or people of the Way. If we try to put ourselves in Paul's place, it makes sense. He was schooled in Judaism since he was a young boy. He had studied with the best and knew the Old Testament scrolls intimately. He, with other faithful Jews, was waiting for Messiah to come and liberate God's people from their oppressors. When Jesus appeared on the scene, he didn't seem like their concept of Messiah. He didn't look like a powerful king who would set his people free. He came from a small, unremarkable town and hung out with fishermen and tax collectors. Then he was arrested and executed as a common criminal. Now his followers were trying to start a revolution. In Paul's mind, it had to be stamped out. It was becoming dangerous.

In chapter 2 we read about the death of Stephen, who was stoned for his faith in Christ. Do you remember where people left their coats as they got ready to join in the stoning?

Meanwhile, the witnesses laid their coats at the feet of a young man named Saul. (Acts 7:58 NIV)

Paul and Saul are the same man. Some people assume that his name was changed after his conversion, but that's not accurate. Saul is his Hebrew name and Paul is his Greek name. After the stoning of Stephen, he became a committed persecutor of the early church. He was a deeply devout man, and he believed that this new group was a cult.

> Meanwhile, Saul was uttering threats with every breath and was eager to kill the Lord's followers. So he went to the high priest. He requested letters addressed to the synagogues in Damascus, asking for their cooperation in the arrest of any followers of the Way he found there. He wanted to bring them—both men and women—back to Jerusalem in chains. (9:1–2)

It was on his way to Damascus that he had an encounter with the risen Christ.

> As he was approaching Damascus on this mission, a light from heaven suddenly shone down around him. He fell to the ground and heard a voice saying to him, "Saul! Saul! Why are you persecuting me?"
> "Who are you, lord?" Saul asked.
> And the voice replied, "I am Jesus, the one you are persecuting!" (vv. 3–5)

When Saul got up off the ground, he was blind. His men had heard a voice, but they didn't see what Saul saw. Unsure what to do next, they led him to a home in Damascus where he could rest and recover. For three days he sat with this new reality. Everything he believed was wrong. Where do you go from there? How do you pray when you discover that the person you believed to be an imposter is actually the Son of God and you missed it? Did he think back to Stephen's stoning and realize that the person whose death he fully endorsed had understood what he had completely missed? God's plan was unfolding in Saul's life and the next piece was about to be put in place.

> Now there was a believer in Damascus named Ananias. The Lord spoke to him in a vision, calling, "Ananias!"
>
> "Yes, Lord!" he replied.
>
> The Lord said, "Go over to Straight Street, to the house of Judas. When you get there, ask for a man from Tarsus named Saul. He is praying to me right now. I have shown him a vision of a man named Ananias coming in and laying hands on him so he can see again."
>
> "But Lord," exclaimed Ananias, "I've heard many people talk about the terrible things this man has done to the believers in Jerusalem! And he is authorized by the leading priests to arrest everyone who calls upon your name."
>
> But the Lord said, "Go, for Saul is my chosen instrument to take my message to the Gentiles and to kings, as well as to the people of Israel." (vv. 10–15)

Ananias was understandably shocked by this request. Jewish believers knew who Saul was. They were afraid of the power he had, and the stories coming out of Jerusalem were terrifying. It would be like asking a Jewish person during World War II to go to a house where Hitler was staying. It was that extreme. Saul was out to eradicate this group, to have them arrested and punished, many killed. But Ananias was a godly man and so he went; he laid hands on Saul and prayed for him to be filled with the Holy Spirit. We read that scales fell off Saul's eyes, his sight was restored, and his life and mission were eternally changed.

There was one more event in Paul's life that we don't know much about, but I believe it helped him endure the many persecutions, stoning, shipwrecks, and betrayals that lay ahead. Not only that, but it also serves as a glorious promise to those of us who are longing for our heavenly home and wondering what that will be like.

Paul Saw Heaven

We touched on this a little earlier as we looked at the three examples we have in Scripture of those who were taken to the third heaven without dying. But there is something else I want us to see that I believe will help us understand why Paul not only longed for heaven but was torn between that and a desire to remain on earth. He writes about it in his second letter to the church in Corinth. It's easy to skim over what life was like in the early church, but just as churches have issues and problems today, so they did in Paul's time. He was writing to a divided church, a church that was challenging his authority as an apostle, and a church where false teachers were leading young, new converts down the wrong path. In chapter 11 he reminds them of all the terrible things that he's had to endure, but then he goes on to share with them something that had taken place fourteen years earlier.

> I was caught up to the third heaven fourteen years ago. Whether I was in my body or out of my body, I don't know—only God knows. Yes, only God knows whether I was in my body or outside my body. But I do know that I was caught up to paradise and heard things so astounding that they cannot be expressed in words, things no human is allowed to tell. (2 Cor. 12:2–4)

I think it's remarkable that Paul had told no one about this experience for fourteen years. We are so used to documenting every moment in our social media world, from what we ate last night to our holiday pictures. Paul was actually in heaven and told no one for fourteen years. He heard things that are only talked about in heaven, not on earth. It's one thing to believe with all your heart that Christ is God's perfect Son and that our eternal home is with him in heaven, but can you imagine what it must have been like to be taken there, to see with your own eyes?

I've often wondered about Paul's "thorn in the flesh," but he made it clear that it was precisely because he'd been to heaven and knew what it's like and heard things that he couldn't talk about that he was given this burden. "So to keep me from becoming proud, I was given a thorn in my flesh, a messenger from Satan to torment me and keep me from becoming proud" (v. 7).

Here's what I think is so fascinating about Paul feeling torn between heaven and earth. With my limited human understanding, I think that if I had ever been in heaven I wouldn't want to come back to earth. If I'd experienced the beauty and the joy and the peace that heaven is, why would I ever want to come back to a place that is often filled with disappointment and heartache?

Paul Saw Hope

What Paul saw and heard in heaven radically changed him. He must have been given an understanding of God's whole plan from the beginning. My thinking that I'd want to stay is a flawed, human response. What Paul must have seen and understood stretched his heart wide open to see God's plan for you and for me. That's what spurred him on to endure everything that he would endure because he understood God's big plan. Heaven has always been God's plan for us. But what Paul saw and understood also gave him the grace and the vision to live here because he knew what waits for us there, and it was his passionate desire to see as many people as possible fall in love with Jesus.

> When Paul tells us that the hope we have will not lead to disappointment, he speaks with the authority of one who had been given the privilege of seeing our hope.

What did Paul see that impacted him so much? What was his experience in heaven like? He was not given permission to share the details with us, but when we read through all his letters to the different churches in the New Testament, we hear his urgent, passionate heart telling us to hold on, to look up.

I press on to reach the end of the race and receive the heavenly prize for which God, through Christ Jesus, is calling us. (Phil. 3:14)

We can rejoice, too, when we run into problems and trials, for we know that they help us develop endurance. And endurance develops strength of character, and character strengthens our confident hope of salvation. And this hope will not lead to disappointment. (Rom. 5:3–5)

We hold on to hope, but Paul saw the hope with his own eyes. When Paul wrote to the church in Philippi, his letter was dripping with joy. The amazing thing about the tone of his letter is that he's in prison as he writes. He is chained night and day to a guard, and yet over and over he writes about experiencing joy as a disciple of Christ. He also writes that he longs for heaven.

For I fully expect and hope that I will never be ashamed, but that I will continue to be bold for Christ, as I have been in the past. And I trust that my life will bring honor to Christ, whether I live or die. For to me, living means living for Christ, and dying is even better. But if I live, I can do more fruitful work for Christ. So I really don't know which is better. I'm torn between two desires: I long to go and be with Christ, which would be far better for me. But for your sakes, it is better that I continue to live. (Phil. 1:20–24)

When Paul tells us that the hope we have will not lead to disappointment, he speaks with the authority of one who had been given the privilege of seeing our hope. That is life-changing.

God Is the Master Creator

I am longing to finally see God. He is such a masterful Creator, breathing new life and energy into every moment. That's not always our experience here on earth.

Let's be honest, we've all been in some boring church services. I heard a story of a guest preacher who had been invited to deliver the message one Sunday morning. The senior pastor remained on the platform after he introduced his guest. He had told him that he had thirty-five minutes to deliver his message, after that the congregation would get antsy. The man preached for thirty-five minutes and kept going. Forty-five minutes, fifty minutes. By the time he hit an hour, the senior pastor was getting desperate trying to signal to him to wrap it up. As all his loud whispers were falling on deaf ears, he picked up a hymnbook and threw it at him. Unfortunately, it missed the preacher and hit a man in the front row, who cried out, "Hit me again. I can still hear him!" I've been in services like that.

One of the greatest challenges to our understanding of how amazing it will be to finally be home with Jesus is what we've experienced here on earth. Let me be clear though, I love church. I believe in church. Christ is returning for his church. But at times we've done a poor job of helping others see a picture of who he is.

The idea that God is boring is outrageous. Think about it. Think of all the beauty you've ever seen—the mountains, the lakes, the sunsets, and the starry nights. God did all of that. Think of the great artists through the years, the architects of all the great cathedrals and buildings. God gave them those gifts. Think of the music and voices that move you deep in your soul. Every note was God's idea. Think of the colors in fall, the reds and golds and burnt orange. They are only a pale shadow of what we will see in heaven. Everything you have ever longed to see and hear and feel will be in your heavenly home. All beauty now is but a shadow of what's to come.

You Will Be Who You Always Longed to Be

One of the most amazing things about being free of sin and struggles will be finally being who God created us to be. Do you ever get tired of yourself? I know I do at times. I get frustrated when I fall into the same old patterns or react in the same old way. I get tired of thinking in the same way. What about you? Whatever it is about yourself that you find frustrating or discouraging will be gone. There will be no more self-doubt or fear or sadness. You'll be the beautiful, creative, joy-filled you that God created you to be.

> But we are citizens of heaven, where the Lord Jesus Christ lives. And we are eagerly waiting for him to return as our Savior. He will take our weak mortal bodies and change them into glorious bodies like his own, using the same power with which he will bring everything under his control. (Phil. 3:20–21)

You'll have a glorious body. No more aching joints or bad hair days. No more falling into bed exhausted at night. I know that we are living in challenging days. You only have to watch five minutes of the evening news to hear story after story of devastation and unrest, of earthquakes and floods, of political manipulation and slander. It can be easy to become discouraged, but that's why we have to remember who we are and where we belong. Paul wrote this letter to a church that was struggling to survive in the Roman colony of Philippi. The primary title that the Romans used for the emperor (who was the evil Emperor Nero at this time) was "lord and savior." Now Paul uses those titles for the only One who deserves them, Jesus Christ our Lord and Savior. He reminds them that no matter what is going on around them our forever home is in heaven.

Keep your eyes fixed on Jesus and look forward to that day when a glorious body will be yours.

We're living in days of increasing blasphemy, but as Paul writes, we are "eagerly waiting" for Jesus to return. Don't let the evil and cynicism of this world get to you. Keep your eyes fixed on Jesus and look forward to that day when a glorious body will be yours. You'll be free from anything that has held you back in this world, ready to soar in the next.

Your Conversations Will Be Life-Giving

Have you ever texted a friend or a loved one and they read the text differently than you meant it to be read? You were simply giving information and somehow they read it as criticism or judgment. That will all be over as well. We'll be able to communicate with one another perfectly, with no misunderstanding. I read this online text exchange and it made me laugh.

"I'm here for you."

"Thank you so much. I've been really struggling recently but no one seems to notice. And, sorry, I've lost all my contacts recently. Who is this?"

"I'm your Uber driver. I'm here to pick you up."

Embarrassing but survivable. But so many relationships have been damaged or lost simply because of a lack of communication. Words can hurt, and when they're spoken in anger or without thought a lot of damage can be done. When we are finally home, there will be no more of those conversations. Perhaps someone has passed, and you were never able to resolve the situation between you. In heaven, all hurt and pain will be gone.

And just think of the conversations you will be able to have.

Can you imagine sitting down with Abraham and talking with him about God showing him the stars in the sky?

What will it be like to talk to David and ask him what it felt like to be anointed as king of Israel when he was just a shepherd boy?

To sit with Peter and listen as he talks about going from a simple fisherman to Peter, the rock?

To thank C. S. Lewis and Tolkien for their marvelous books and perhaps get to read what they are writing now?

To listen to what Bach and Handel are composing and look at the new works of art from Rembrandt?

To rejoice with Billy Graham at the number of people who are there because he stayed faithful to his calling?

Jonathan Edwards is best known for his message "Sinners in the Hands of an Angry God." This powerful sermon was the catalyst for the first Great Awakening that took place in the eighteenth century, but it's one of his lesser-known works that I love. It's a small book called *Heaven, A World of Love*. This is what he wrote about what heaven will be like:

> There will be no such things as flattery or insincerity in Heaven, but there, perfect sincerity will reign through all in all. Everyone will be just what he seems to be and will really have all the love he seems to have. It will not be as it is in this earth where comparatively few things are what they seem to be and where professions are often made lightly and without meaning. But there, every expression of love shall come from the bottom of the heart, and all that is professed shall be really and truly felt.[1]

Can you imagine how wonderful that will be? Every moment of every day we will be perfectly loved. No more questioning and wondering or second guessing, just loved.

Your Work Will Be What You've Always Longed to Do

I've had a job since I was fourteen years old. Now, obviously at that young age my job was restricted to Saturdays and summer holidays. I've been a maid in a hotel, and I've worked as a waitress. (I didn't last long as a waitress as I tended to steer people clear of dishes that looked a little dodgy to me.) I've worked in a record store, I've been a contemporary Christian artist, worked as a television host with the BBC in London, and hosted talk shows here in the US. I've honestly enjoyed all my jobs, but there's been a common thread that I wonder if you relate to. Even the jobs I've loved the most have just a little something missing, something that's not quite what I hoped for. Not only that, but they're also tiring. I'm sure you can relate. Work is good, it's necessary, but it's hard.

Here's the great news about heaven. As I've mentioned earlier, we won't be floating around on clouds plucking a harp, but neither will we be in a heavenly recliner waiting for the next service to begin. We will have jobs, assignments, creative outlets in heaven, but they won't wear us out. We'll be doing what we've always dreamt of, but we won't get tired. Work that's exhausting was a result of the fall. Before that, work was never supposed to be hard. Adam was given the job of tending to the beautiful garden that God made.

Life was beautiful, effortless in Eden. There was work to do but it was productive and rewarding. That all changed with the fall. God made it clear to Adam that the work he used to love, which was easy and fulfilling, would now be hard work.

> Since you listened to your wife and ate from the tree
>> whose fruit I commanded you not to eat,
> the ground is cursed because of you.
>> All your life you will struggle to scratch a living from it.
> It will grow thorns and thistles for you,
>> though you will eat of its grains.
> By the sweat of your brow
>> will you have food to eat
> until you return to the ground
>> from which you were made. (Gen. 3:17–19)

Eden must have been so breathtakingly beautiful before the fall. We will see its beauty again.

Your Longings Will Be Fulfilled

There are many people who have sacrificed their hopes and dreams to take care of others. My mum left school when she was sixteen to help her mother care for her father, who had Alzheimer's. She had always dreamt of being a teacher. I won't be a bit surprised if she is a teacher in heaven. I wonder what unfulfilled dreams, things you sacrificed for others, are still tucked inside of you. Perhaps you started something and simply didn't have the time to complete it. Life interrupted. Or an illness shelved your gifts. You are still you, with the same heart and desires, but your body simply won't allow you to carry on. I believe that in heaven, with a new body and new strength, you will be given a wide-open heaven to explore every God-given dream you've ever had.

> I used to try to erase that feeling deep inside, that ache for something more, but now I embrace it. It should be there. We were made for more.

Not only will we be able to use all the gifts and talents that God has deposited in each one of us, we'll actually get to serve alongside the angels. I think that will be amazing. Toward the end of the revelation given to John, we read,

> And the angel said to me, "Write this: Blessed are those who are invited to the wedding feast of the Lamb." And he added, "These are true words that come from God."
>
> Then I fell down at his feet to worship him, but he said, "No, don't worship me. I am a servant of God, just like you and your brothers and sisters who testify about their faith in Jesus. Worship only God." (Rev. 19:9–10)

Won't that be amazing to serve with the angels? What life awaits each one of us when that longing that exists in every human heart is finally satisfied? When we get home, we will understand what we've been longing for. I used to try to erase that feeling deep inside, that ache for something more, but now I embrace it. It should be there. We were made for more, and he has planted eternity in every human heart. That is why you long for more. God placed it in you.

Yet God has made everything beautiful for its own time. He has planted eternity in the human heart, but even so, people cannot see the whole scope of God's work from beginning to end. (Eccles. 3:11)

We innately know that the suffering and sorrow we see around us shouldn't be there. Every time we read of a child struggling with an incurable disease or someone struck down in the prime of their life, there is more than sorrow there, there is a soul-cry of "No! Why?"

Our brother Paul, who had been to heaven, who had seen what we long to see, wrote to encourage us in the midst of discouragements and struggles not to give up but to look up.

That is why we never give up. Though our bodies are dying, our spirits are being renewed every day. For our present troubles are small and won't last very long. Yet they produce for us a glory that vastly outweighs them and will last forever! So we don't look at the troubles we can see now; rather, we fix our gaze on things that cannot be seen. For the things we see now will soon be gone, but the things we cannot see will last forever. (2 Cor. 4:16–18)

Since childhood, I've been a huge fan of almost everything C. S. Lewis has written but in particular *The Chronicles of Narnia*. In the seventh and last book of the series, there is a beautiful depiction of what it will be like to finally reach heaven and realize that it is what we have been longing for all our lives. I love the sentiment he shares through the Unicorn, who stamps his hoof and says that he is home at last. That is what I think we will all say, that we are home at last. That it is what we have always been longing for. We may not have words for it now, but once we are home, we will recognize it. Eternity with Christ is where we have always belonged.

> **Eternity with Christ is where we have always belonged.**

Think of all the best moments in your life. Every single one of them is a promise of what is to come!

Father God,
   I can't wait. I can't wait until I am finally home and see you in all your glory and live the life you have always had for me.
   Because of Jesus,
   Amen.

What I Know about Heaven

When I get home, every longing in my heart will be fulfilled.

7

ARE THERE
REWARDS IN HEAVEN?

Look, I am coming soon, bringing my reward with me to repay all people
according to their deeds. I am the Alpha and the Omega, the First and
the Last, the Beginning and the End.

Revelation 22:12–13

It was one of the most cringeworthy moments I've ever seen
on television. I was flipping through channels one evening and
paused as I realized I had caught the very end of the Miss Universe beauty pageant, and they were about to announce the winner.
I'm not usually into pageants but, as it was the finale, I decided
to stay and watch. There were two women in glamorous evening
gowns, center stage, facing one another and holding hands. Both
women were stunningly beautiful, Miss Colombia and Miss Philippines. Steve Harvey was the host for the evening, and he walked
onto the stage holding the official white card to announce the

results. Tension was in the air as he paused for a few seconds before announcing.

"Miss Universe 2015 is . . . Colombia!"[1]

The crowd erupted in cheers as the two women embraced and Miss Philippines left the stage. A beautiful crown was placed on Miss Colombia's head as she waved to the audience, acknowledging their applause, holding a small Colombian flag in the air. I was about to continue flipping channels, looking for the Food Network, when I saw Steve Harvey, who had left the stage as Miss Colombia was being crowned, return to center stage. He looked troubled.

"I have to apologize. The first runner-up is Colombia. Miss Universe 2015 is Miss Philippines."

It was an absolutely shocking moment. He had accidentally read the first name he saw, which was not the winner but the first runner-up. The cameras panned to Miss Philippines at the side of the stage as she was directed to come forward and receive her crown. Miss Colombia looked stunned, unsure of what had just happened until the previous year's winner removed the crown that had just been placed on her head and put it on the head of Miss Philippines. The whole thing was a mess. The audience was now booing at the confusion and mix-up. It was terrible. The joy of being announced as the winner only to have that snatched away in front of a live audience and broadcast around the world must have been devastating. A moment of glory tainted for both women.

We are a culture that thrives on awards. If you think about it, apart from beauty pageants we have the Oscars, the Grammys, the People's Choice Awards, the Tonys, the Golden Globes, the Country Music Awards, the Super Bowl, the Heisman Trophy, the Stanley Cup, the U.S. Open. The list goes on and on. Receiving an award like that is wonderful. It's an acknowledgment from your peers that you are the best at what you do at that moment in time. I've received a few awards through the years, and although I'm grateful, those moments are fleeting. They are not eternal. But let me ask you this, did you realize that when we are home with Christ there will be an award show like nothing this world has ever seen? If Christ gives you an award, no one can ever take it away.

The Only Awards That Matter

We've looked in the previous chapters at the biblical truths about heaven and answered some of the most important questions. In this section, I want us to look at how the hope of heaven impacts the life that we have now, here on earth. When you begin to understand the absolute joy that lies ahead, it shapes our days on earth. There's some wonderful news ahead for us.

Did you know that every believer will stand before the judgment seat of Christ, not to be punished but to be rewarded? This is so important to me. I want you to understand that this will happen. Your life matters. Everything you do for Christ, whether anyone on earth notices or not, God does. I have met hundreds of people through the years who are quietly serving God, showing up in ways that are seldom recognized, but I know that their day is coming when Christ himself will reward them. I want that to be you!

We don't get to choose who is born with a beautiful singing voice, or who is a math whiz or a brilliant engineer. We don't get to decide how tall we are or what family we're born into, but we do get to choose how we live each day for Christ.

Earthly awards are here for a moment and then put on a shelf and forgotten. (Did you know that if you win an Academy Award and then decide to sell it, you have to offer it back to the Academy first? You get $10. Hard to retire on that.) We spend so much of our lives worrying about our careers, our bank accounts, our physical appearance. If you get them all lined up just the way you want them, you've got them for probably seventy or eighty years. Yet if we spend our lives truly laying up treasure in heaven, it will last for eternity. I wish I could write this whole chapter in bold type and capitalize every word because this can be life-changing stuff for every one of us.

Do you ever find yourself thinking that life is not fair?

Why do I always feel disappointed?

Why is nothing ever as great as I think it will be?

Why do I feel anxious all the time?

Why am I sick?

Why did she find a husband?

Why did my marriage not work out?

Why did he get that promotion?

Why are their kids doing so well?

Why can't I afford a house like that?

Why don't I ever feel like enough?

Whatever it is that feels inequitable to you, hold on. Your real life is coming, and when you choose to live your life on earth for Jesus, your eternal reward will blow anything on this earth away. You might be tempted to ask, "Who will need a reward in heaven? Surely being there with Christ is enough." I would agree, but this is not my idea, it's his. I'm going to give you as much scriptural content here as I can find so that you don't think I'm exaggerating the promise. I don't need to. It's amazing.

> **This world is not fair, it is broken, it is hard, but when you place your trust and your eternal life in Jesus's hands, all will be well.**

Let's unpack one of those passages, and then we'll look at the multitude of verses we've been given. I'm serious here. This could change your life forever. This world is not fair, it is broken, it is hard, but when you place your trust and your eternal life in Jesus's hands, all will be well.

Jesus Is the Firm Foundation

The only lasting foundation for any of our lives is one built on Christ. Paul made that clear when he wrote to the church in Corinth that was facing all sorts of problems.

> For no one can lay any foundation other than the one we already have—Jesus Christ. Anyone who builds on that foundation may use a variety of materials—gold, silver, jewels, wood, hay, or straw. But on judgment day, fire will reveal what kind of work each builder has done. The fire will show if a person's work has any value. If the work survives, that builder will receive a reward. But if the work is burned up, the builder will suffer great loss. The builder will be saved, but like someone barely escaping through a wall of flames. (1 Cor. 3:11–15)

First of all, the correct interpretation of this passage is that Paul is writing to those who are leaders in the church in Corinth. He is encouraging those who are continuing the work of building up the church he started to make sure that they are building with the right stuff. It is serious business to be entrusted with the leadership of God's people.

The application for you and me, however, is this: How do we build our lives in such a way that they have an eternal impact? Let's put this passage in context. This is Paul's first letter to the church in Corinth, which is in southern Greece, and he's writing to try to straighten out a few things. There's a lot of jealousy and division in the church that's stunting its growth. Corinth was a very wealthy, flashy city, a bit like Las Vegas. It was known as a place where you could rightly say, "Whatever happens in Corinth, stays in Corinth." It was a busy seaport, known for immorality, idol worship (particularly Aphrodite, goddess of love), and a laissez-faire attitude of anything goes. Strabo, who was a Greek historian at that time, wrote this about Corinth:

> And the temple of Aphrodite was so rich that it owned more than a thousand temple slaves, courtesans, whom both men and women

had dedicated to the goddess. And therefore, it was also on account of these women that the city was crowded with people and grew rich; for instance, the ship captains freely squandered their money, and hence the proverb, "Not for every man is the voyage to Corinth."[2]

I quote the above to make a point. It's tempting to look at the world we live in and think, things have never been this bad, we are living in the evilest of days. History would speak to that. Yes, there are biblical signs that point to the reality that we are living in the last days, but human history tells a compellingly similar story through the centuries about our fallen human nature. Without Christ, without the grace of God, culture falls apart and anything is possible and becomes permissible.

It's to the church in that city that Paul writes this first letter and in particular, the passage we are looking at: "For no one can lay any foundation other than the one we already have" (1 Cor. 3:11).

One of the first issues that Paul addresses before he writes about work that will last is the division that's happening in the church. The church has become polarized. Some members are saying they're not following Paul, they're following Apollos, and vice versa. Apollos was a friend, a contemporary of Paul, a fellow evangelist who carried on Paul's work in Corinth. Paul had spent eighteen months in Corinth getting the church established, and after he moved on, Apollos followed up. Others in the church were saying they're not Apollos's people, they're Paul's. I have to believe that being a church pastor has got to be one of the most challenging callings ever. Let's face it. We, the church, we're hard work. What Paul is trying to help them see here is that it's all the same work no matter who starts it or who carries it on. Some of us plant seeds and some get to water them, but the only one who can take credit for the growth is God. These issues are still rampant in our churches. Someone starts a church and then a new team comes along and follows up and sees great growth. It's in our fallen human nature to take sides and decide who should get the credit. Only one should get the credit—Christ alone.

Have you ever had to wrestle with issues like this? Perhaps you've served in your church for a long time and then someone else comes along and gets a position that you feel you're entitled to. Or in your career or in your small group, it's very easy for jealousy to fester. It's not a sin to feel that way, but it is a sin to allow it to take root. Emotions themselves are not sinful; it's what we do with them that matters.

Social media has made this so much worse. We look at where someone is and who they're with and we want to know why we weren't invited. What did we do wrong to be excluded? Why is their following so much bigger than ours? It's the duty of a responsible leader to constantly point back to Jesus. We are not called to gather a following for ourselves; we are called to teach others how to follow Jesus. If any leader is attempting to build

> **Emotions themselves are not sinful; it's what we do with them that matters.**

an audience for themselves, they have not only missed their calling, but they have also strayed onto holy ground that belongs to God alone.

I'll be honest, I've had to wrestle with these things. I'll release a book at the same time as some of my friends, and when one of theirs does incredibly well, I wonder what I could have done better, said better, written better. I've been nominated for two Grammys, and when it wasn't my name that was called out there was a moment's twinge of wishing it had been me. (I did win a Dove Award one year for best international artist, but let me say this: I was the only international artist in the US at the time, and not only that, but they also spelled my name wrong!) All that to say, this is human nature.

But what Paul is reminding the leaders in Corinth and reminding us too is that it doesn't matter what role we play, how we serve,

> **We need to keep our eyes fixed on Jesus because Jesus has his eyes fixed on us.**

or who notices; what matters is that we do our part knowing that God is the one who made it all work. When a church is thriving under servant leadership, Christ gets the glory. This is important because further on in this passage Paul is going to talk about work that will last eternally. But he wants to make it clear that we need to keep our eyes fixed on Jesus because Jesus has his eyes fixed on us.

The Eternal Foundation

Anyone who builds on that foundation may use a variety of materials—gold, silver, jewels, wood, hay, or straw. (1 Cor. 3:12)

What's immediately clear about the above list is that three of those things are precious and will last and three are commonplace and will not. Although Paul is specifically addressing the leaders in Corinth in this passage, he does address "anyone who builds." We are all building something, whether it's a church, a business, or a family. We are living in days when people are watering down the truth of the gospel. Before his execution, Jesus warned about this. Two days before Passover, he sat down with his disciples on the Mount of Olives and told them about things that were going to happen.

And many will turn away from me and betray and hate each other. And many false prophets will appear and will deceive many people. Sin will be rampant everywhere, and the love of many will grow cold. (Matt. 24:10–12)

We see that all around us now. People who once claimed to know Jesus are walking away from their faith, and behavior that Scripture clearly calls sinful is embraced as the new normal. It's clear that the love of many is growing cold. So what are we building our lives with? Are we building on things that can be destroyed in a moment or on things that will last forever?

Visiting Israel for the first time was life-changing. The Bible came alive before my eyes. Stories that I'd once known, suddenly put in context, became so real. I've known the story that Jesus told about the wise and foolish builders since I was a child.

> Anyone who listens to my teaching and follows it is wise, like a person who builds a house on solid rock. Though the rain comes in torrents and the floodwaters rise and the winds beat against that house, it won't collapse because it is built on bedrock. But anyone who hears my teaching and doesn't obey it is foolish, like a person who builds a house on sand. When the rains and floods come and the winds beat against that house, it will collapse with a mighty crash. (Matt. 7:24–27)

We even had a song about it, remember? "The Wise Man Built His House upon the Rock."

As I was out walking one day with my Jewish guide, we crossed over a dried-up riverbed. I asked him if it was always like this, and he told me that when the rain comes, this dried-up riverbed floods in minutes. There's very little warning. The story suddenly made so much more sense. When we build our lives on Jesus and on the rock-solid bed of his Word, then it doesn't matter what kind of storm hits our lives. Because we're built on him, we stand. When we build with a flawed, faulty foundation of wood, hay, and stubble and a storm hits, we're done. It's tempting to isolate these days, but we need to connect

When we build our lives on Jesus and on the rock-solid bed of his Word, then it doesn't matter what kind of storm hits our lives. Because we're built on him, we stand.

with God through prayer and spending time in his Word. Then we need to find a loving community of God's people who will be there for us when life gets stormy. That will give us a firm foundation.

Our Lives Fully Revealed

> The fire will show if a person's work has any value. If the work survives, that builder will receive a reward. (1 Cor. 3:13–14)

I love this story told by missionary Amy Carmichael.

> One day we took the children to see a goldsmith refine gold after the ancient manner of the East. He was sitting beside his little charcoal fire. ("He shall sit as a refiner"; the gold- or silversmith never leaves his crucible once it is on the fire.) In the red glow lay a common curved roof tile; another tile covered it like a lid. This was the crucible. In it was the medicine made of salt, tamarind fruit and burnt brick dust, and imbedded in it was the gold. The medicine does its appointed work on the gold, "then the fire eats it," and the goldsmith lifts the gold out with a pair of tongs, lets it cool, rubs it between his fingers, and if not satisfied puts it back again in fresh medicine. This time he blows the fire hotter than it was before, and each time he puts the gold into the crucible, the heat of the fire is increased; "it could not bear it so hot at first, but it can bear it now; what would have destroyed it then helps it now." "How do you know when the gold is purified?" we asked him, and he answered, "When I can see my face in it [the liquid gold in the crucible] then it is pure."[3]

What a powerful illustration. That's my prayer. It's a dangerous prayer to pray, but I want to be so refined that the Father can see his face in my life. Paul makes it clear that some things can survive a fire, whereas others cannot. That can read as an overwhelming challenge or as an encouragement to stay close to Jesus and build our lives on him. The fire that Paul is writing about, in this context, is not seen as something that purifies but rather as something that reveals. On the day of judgment, our lives will be fully revealed. Paul continues,

> But if the work is burned up, the builder will suffer great loss. The builder will be saved, but like someone barely escaping through a wall of flames. (1 Cor. 3:15)

This can be a confusing passage if we don't understand what Paul is saying. What will this great loss be? This does not refer to our salvation. Our salvation is built on one thing and one thing alone: our faith in Jesus Christ. That is clear over and over in Scripture. If you have placed your trust in Christ and the sacrifice he made for you on the cross, you never have to fear judgment.

> He does not punish us for all our sins;
>   he does not deal harshly with us, as we deserve.
> For his unfailing love toward those who fear him
>   is as great as the height of the heavens above the earth.
> He has removed our sins as far from us
>   as the east is from the west. (Ps. 103:10–12)

> So now there is no condemnation for those who belong to Christ Jesus. And because you belong to him, the power of the life-giving Spirit has freed you from the power of sin that leads to death. (Rom. 8:1–2)

Christ paid for our sins on the cross. As noted previously, when he cried out, "It is finished," our sin debt, past, present, and future, was paid for. If you ever feel ashamed or condemned, I want you to know that is never from God. The Holy Spirit brings conviction, which draws us closer to Jesus, but never condemnation.

So what is Paul warning us about? What can be lost? What he is describing has to do with how we live our lives once we have surrendered them to Christ. No one whose name is in the Lamb's Book of Life will ever face the Great White Throne Judgment. If that term is new to you, that judgment is reserved for those who until the very moment of their death refuse to acknowledge and surrender their lives to Jesus. What many Christians don't understand, however, is that each one of us will stand before the judgment seat of Christ. The original Greek term is directly translated "bema seat." This is a term and a picture that would have been familiar to Paul's Grecian audience in Corinth. In the large Olympian arenas where games were played, the bema was a seat set up above the crowd. This is where the judge would sit, and it was never about punishment, it was all about rewards. It was where the winning athletes came to be given their medals.

> **There is nothing, absolutely nothing, more important than how we will spend eternity.**

> For we must all stand before Christ to be judged. We will each receive whatever we deserve for the good or evil we have done in this earthly body. (2 Cor. 5:10)

There are many things in our lives that we have little control over. We raise our children to love God. We teach them what God's Word says. But at some point, they head off to college or move out into their profession, and then we do most of our work on our knees in prayer, trusting that God is with them.

You work hard in your profession, go above and beyond, work harder than the guy next to you, but ultimately you have little control over who gets the promotion.

You're single and someone new enters your friend group. You are very attracted to him or her, but you have little control over whether that feeling is reciprocated.

Life can be very frustrating in all the areas where we feel we have no control, but when it comes to your eternal life, you get to choose. This is amazing to me. There is nothing, absolutely nothing, more important than how we will spend eternity.

The idea of rewards is not isolated to the New Testament. It was a concept well understood in the Old Testament as well.

> May the Lord, the God of Israel, under whose wings you have come to take refuge, reward you fully for what you have done. (Ruth 2:12)

> Then at last everyone will say, "There truly is a reward for those who live for God; surely there is a God who judges justly here on earth." (Ps. 58:11)

In the Sermon on the Mount Jesus said,

> God blesses you when people mock you and persecute you and lie about you and say all sorts of evil things against you because you are my followers. Be happy about it! Be very glad! For a great reward awaits you in heaven. (Matt. 5:11–12)

As we saw at the beginning of this chapter,

> Look, I am coming soon, bringing my reward with me to repay all people according to their deeds. I am the Alpha and the Omega, the First and the Last, the Beginning and the End. (Rev. 22:12–13)

What Will the Rewards Be?

I don't get back to Scotland as often as I would like to. When my mum was alive, I'd fly home every second year, and it was on one of those trips that I was given an unusual "reward." A Scottish pastor saw on my social media that I was going to be visiting my mum and wrote to ask if I would like to do an event one evening in his church. I said that I would love to. He asked if it would cost him anything (a true Scot), and I assured him that it would not.

Mum and I took the train north that day, did a little shopping, and in the late afternoon we made our way to his church. The pastor was very kind and told me that they had done a lot of advertising, and they were expecting a full house. Sure enough, the church was packed. I really enjoyed having an opportunity to be with a Scottish congregation again.

At the close of my message, as I was about to leave the platform, the pastor came up and joined me. He announced that they were going to take up a love offering. I was surprised as I didn't expect them to do anything like that. He bowed his head to pray before the offering was taken and then he said, "Don't worry. Sheila Walsh won't see a penny of it! It'll be staying right here in the church."

He then presented me with a rather sad-looking plant, which he apologized for, saying that it fell off the passenger seat in his car, landed upside down, and may have been "stood on a bit." Mum and I laughed the whole way home on the train.

I'm pretty sure that there will be no sad-looking plants in heaven . . . but what are the rewards that Christ will give us?

The Victor's Crown

One of the things that Paul must have experienced in the eighteen months that he was in Corinth was the intense preparation for the Greco-Roman Isthmian Games. These games were held in the spring for athletes. The various events included chariot races, boxing, and foot races. Paul used an illustration that was very familiar to his audience to say if these athletes were willing to train so hard for a prize that wouldn't last (usually a crown of dried wild celery—my sad plant's looking better by the minute), how much more should we run our race and discipline ourselves to win the victor's crown.

Don't you realize that in a race everyone runs, but only one person gets the prize? So run to win! All athletes are disciplined in their training. They do it to win a prize that will fade away, but we do it for an eternal prize. So I run with purpose in every step. I am not just shadowboxing. I discipline my body like an athlete, training it to do what it should. Otherwise, I fear that after preaching to others I myself might be disqualified. (1 Cor. 9:24–27)

So, what does that look like? It means doing the right thing whether you feel like it or not. It might mean dragging yourself out of bed on a Sunday morning to be in church rather than turning over and going back to sleep. It might mean saying no to something that you know only serves to pull you away from Jesus. For me, at times it means consciously praising God when I don't feel like it, when depression feels weighty. It might mean picking up the Word of God more often, reaching out to help someone, choosing to be kind, saying a huge "Yes!" to Jesus. More than this, it is finishing the race well. It's easy to get discouraged and tired. I'm sure you've been there. You might be there right now, but I encourage you to keep your eyes fixed on Jesus. Keep running your race. The great news is that we don't struggle to do all this by ourselves. The Holy Spirit is our helper. God's grace and love help us. I promise you, when you cross that finish line, it will be worth it all.

The Crown of Rejoicing

It's very clear from his letter to the believers in Thessalonica how much Paul loves them. In fact, he says that he loved them so much that he shared not just the gospel with them but his very life (1 Thess. 2:8). They are a great joy to him.

After all, what gives us hope and joy, and what will be our proud reward and crown as we stand before our Lord Jesus when he returns? It is you! (1 Thess. 2:19)

The crown of rejoicing is also referred to as the soul-winner's crown. Solomon wrote in Proverbs that the one who does this is wise.

The fruit of the righteous is a tree of life, and whoever captures souls is wise. (Prov. 11:30 ESV)

I know that it can be very intimidating for many people to share their faith with someone else. I was brought up in a strict Scottish Baptist tradition where we were expected to go out onto the streets and tell people about Jesus. Honestly, it was a great training ground for me, although I'm sure I annoyed a lot of people. I learned to listen as much as talk.

Now I feel differently about talking about Jesus. He is without a doubt my best friend. I love him so much, and it's only natural that he comes up in my conversations. It is not my job to convince anyone about who Jesus is—only the Holy Spirit can do that—but it's one of the greatest gifts in life when someone asks you to help them find their way home.

Is there someone in your circle of influence who has been on your heart for a while? Have there been moments when you felt as if you could have shared your love for Jesus but held back as you didn't want to offend the person or damage your relationship? Have you considered that this might be God prompting you, letting you know that they might be ready to receive the best news they have ever heard? Don't be afraid to reach out. There are no perfect words or formulas, just opportunities to tell someone about the greatest love you've ever known. I still remember the first person I had an opportunity to talk to about Jesus. I was fourteen years old, we were friends, and when she finally asked me to pray with her, it was one of the best moments in my life. Ask God to guide you, and then be open to watch him use you. It's amazing!

The Crown of Righteousness

For I am already being poured out as a drink offering, and the time of my departure has come. I have fought the good fight, I have finished the race, I have kept the faith. Henceforth there is laid up for me the crown of righteousness, which the Lord, the righteous judge, will award to me on that day, and not only to me but also to all who have loved his appearing. (2 Tim. 4:6–8 ESV)

We can hear in Paul's voice here that he knows his life is almost over. It's believed that this is the last letter he wrote shortly before he was beheaded, probably in the infamous Mamertine Prison in Rome. The prison was originally constructed as a water cistern, but the Romans used it for high-profile criminals on death row. Tradition suggests that both Paul and Peter were held there before their executions. I have to confess that as I read these words by our brother who had suffered so much, I had tears pouring down my cheeks. He had everything thrown at him. He was shipwrecked more than once, he was in prison more than once, he was beaten to within an inch of his life, and so much more (see 2 Cor. 11:25–30), but he was able to say, "I have fought the good fight, I have finished the race, I have kept the faith" (2 Tim. 4:7 ESV). Where did his strength come from? Clearly, he relied on the comfort of the Holy Spirit, but more than that, like Jesus, he had his eyes fixed on home. He kept his gaze on heaven.

Looking to Jesus, the founder and perfecter of our faith, who for the joy that was set before him endured the cross, despising the shame, and is seated at the right hand of the throne of God. (Heb. 12:2 ESV)

I know that it's easy to become discouraged. Life is so . . . daily. That's why it's so important to remember that we are not home. We don't belong here. When you get frustrated, when life drives you crazy, pause for a moment and remember that Jesus told us it would be like this.

I have told you all this so that you may have peace in me. Here on earth you will have many trials and sorrows. But take heart, because I have overcome the world. (John 16:33)

The present can be challenging but the future is secure. My mother was an ardent believer in having something to look forward to. It didn't have to be something huge, but she always had something that she was anticipating. Psychologists tell us that it is healing to our souls to look forward to something. For me now, that is heaven. Every morning when I take Maggie for her walk, I find myself looking up, looking forward to that day when I will finally be home.

The Crown of Life

God blesses those who patiently endure testing and temptation. Afterward they will receive the crown of life that God has promised to those who love him. (James 1:12)

In 2015, twenty-one young Christian men were marched along a beach in Libya and beheaded. Those who were able to watch the video that was put on social media (I could not) said that the last words on the lips of these young men were, "Oh, Lord Jesus." The other thing that struck everyone who watched was the look of calm on their faces. Their executioners, all dressed in black, did everything they could to instill fear, but the peace of Christ rested on each one. When I think of the multitudes through the years who have lost their lives because of their faith, I remember this verse in Revelation:

And they have defeated him by the blood of the Lamb and by their testimony. And they did not love their lives so much that they were afraid to die. (Rev. 12:11)

At this moment, Christians all over the world are enduring horrific persecution in North Korea, Afghanistan, India, Ethiopia, Iran,

China, Nigeria, Sudan, and many more places. Christ has promised them the crown of life.

The Crown of Glory

Don't lord it over the people assigned to your care, but lead them by your own good example. And when the Great Shepherd appears, you will receive a crown of never-ending glory and honor. (1 Pet. 5:3–4)

This crown seems to be particularly for Christian leaders, but I don't think it's only for the pastor of a church. You might lead a Bible study or a small group, you might be a youth group leader or a teacher. I think of so many people who serve faithfully year after year without complaining and with little reward. God misses nothing. When you tenderly care for those who look to you just as we look to Christ, the Great Shepherd who cares for each one of us, there is a crown waiting for you.

What Will We Do with Our Crowns?

I think the most beautiful thing about the crowns given as rewards in heaven is what those who receive them will be able to do with them. It is the only thing that could be done.

The twenty-four elders fall down and worship the one sitting on the throne (the one who lives forever and ever). And they lay their crowns before the throne and say,

"You are worthy, O Lord our God,
    to receive glory and honor and power.
For you created all things,
    and they exist because you created what you pleased."
        (Rev. 4:10–11)

We will do the same. We will cast our crowns at the feet of the only One who is worthy, Jesus. In my younger years as a Christian, I was a great note-taker. If anyone said anything about something that we could do to serve and honor God, I wrote it down. I was determined to be a good Christian. It took me years to understand that we are not saved or loved any more by the things we do. It's all grace.

God saved you by his grace when you believed. And you can't take credit for this; it is a gift from God. Salvation is not a reward for the good things we have done, so none of us can boast about it. For we are God's masterpiece. He has created us anew in Christ Jesus, so we can do the good things he planned for us long ago. (Eph. 2:8–10)

It's all about Jesus. It's all about everything he has done for us. Knowing that makes me want to live in such a way that I look like a daughter of the King. There will be a day when you and I will stand before Jesus. We will see him face-to-face and give an account of the lives we have lived. Let us, as sons and daughters of the King, make that a day of absolute joy!

Dear Father,
I ask in Jesus's name that you would give me the grace and strength to keep the faith, to live my life to honor you, and to finish my race well.
In Jesus's name,
Amen.

What I Know about Heaven

Because I have placed my trust in him, my salvation is eternally secure. One day I will have the joy of standing before the judgment seat of Christ, my Savior and my Lord.

8

WHEN WILL THERE BE A NEW HEAVEN AND A NEW EARTH?

Then I saw a new heaven and a new earth, for the old heaven and the old earth had disappeared. And the sea was also gone. And I saw the holy city, the new Jerusalem, coming down from God out of heaven like a bride beautifully dressed for her husband.

I heard a loud shout from the throne, saying, "Look, God's home is now among his people! He will live with them, and they will be his people. God himself will be with them. He will wipe every tear from their eyes, and there will be no more death or sorrow or crying or pain. All these things are gone forever."

Revelation 21:1–4

It was time for a new home and a new life. At eighteen, our son Christian was accepted into Texas A&M University. It's an amazing school with over seventy-four thousand students. We were very proud. We were also relieved, as being an in-state school means we didn't have to sell our kidneys to send him there. With Christian out of the house for four years, and then going on to graduate school, we decided that it was time for Barry and me to downsize our house. We were now empty nesters. We sold our home in Frisco, Texas, and chose to rent for a while in Dallas until we decided where we might settle long-term. We found a lovely townhome (yes, the one from chapter 1), and even though it was half the size of our previous house, most of our furniture fit. (We had chosen to live in a larger home during all of Christian's middle and high school years as we had determined to make ours the fun home, where all his friends could sleep over or hold parties and just generally hang. We knew that once he was in college, we could get new carpet but we'd never get those years back.)

There's something lovely about moving into a new place. Everything was freshly painted and clean. I loved it all, but I was particularly enamored with the pantry. It was a walk-in pantry with five shelves. Five! I had a soup shelf, a pasta, rice, and condiments shelf, a coffee and tea shelf, a medicine shelf, and one for whatever surprises life might throw at us. I took a photo of it and considered sending it to *Good Housekeeping* magazine but wasn't sure that they had a "Best Pantry in America" section. All was well until it all went terribly wrong.

One of our friends sent us a huge fruit basket to welcome us to our new home. Once we'd finished the fruit, I washed the basket out and put it in the bottom of the pantry to use for some future crafty endeavor (no idea why as I don't have a crafty bone in my body) or perhaps a tool kit for Barry. He only has two tools, a hammer and a screwdriver, but one has to start somewhere.

It was Monday morning, at least that's how I remember it. I was in the kitchen waiting for the coffee to brew and I noticed a few little flies flitting around. I got a tea towel and swatted at them. By Wednesday, they were everywhere, particularly in my potentially award-winning pantry. I determined that they were fruit flies, but we had no fruit left in the house and I didn't know where they were coming from. The flies were multiplying like rabbits. By this time Barry and I both had fly swatters and looked like demented hunters.

We put out dishes of apple cider vinegar and dish soap, a cure offered online, but nothing was helping. Finally, as most of them seemed to be coming from the pantry, we took everything out, emptied every shelf one by one, all five levels!

And there it was. In the very bottom was the offending breeding ground under a twelve-pack of paper towels. A few weeks earlier I had purchased a huge bag of potatoes, used some, and left the rest in the basket. There it was. The original host, a potato that had split in two. I later discovered this disgusting fact: a single rotting potato forgotten at the bottom of a closet or pantry can breed thousands of fruit flies. One little potato had rotted and given birth to our very own Egyptian plague. It's amazing how one wrong thing can contaminate everything. That's not just the story of my pantry; it's the story of every single one of us on earth. One wrong thing changed everything on earth for all of us. Not only for us but for the very earth.

Where Did It All Begin to Go Wrong?

That's all it took. One sin. One act of disobedience to infect everything.

> Since you listened to your wife and ate from the tree whose fruit I commanded you not to eat, the ground is cursed because of you. All your life you will struggle to scratch a living from it. It will grow thorns and thistles for you, though you will eat of its grains. (Gen. 3:17–18)

The earth was never supposed to be as it is now. There were never supposed to be earthquakes and famines, floods and natural disasters. We call them "natural," but that was never God's original intent. Not only do we groan and long for life to be as it was before the fall, but all of creation does also.

> For all creation is waiting eagerly for that future day when God will reveal who his children really are. Against its will, all creation was

subjected to God's curse. But with eager hope, the creation looks forward to the day when it will join God's children in glorious freedom from death and decay. For we know that all creation has been groaning as in the pains of childbirth right up to the present time. (Rom. 8:19–22)

But God

Against its will, creation was subjected to the curse. The very earth that once only gave birth to beauty and life-giving nourishment now gave birth to death and decay. The curse tainted everything . . . but God. I love those two words, *but God*. God had a plan. We see the beginnings of it even as early as Genesis 3, where God made clothes to cover Adam and Eve from the skins of animals.

And the LORD God made clothing from animal skins for Adam and his wife. (Gen. 3:21)

The first drops of blood shed in Eden. The first signs of the scarlet thread that is woven throughout Scripture pointing to that ultimate day when Christ, the Second Adam, would undo the curse once and for all. I'm sure the serpent, Satan, thought he'd won in the garden. He thought he'd won on the cross, but God always had a perfect plan in place. Christ rose from the dead and ascended back into heaven, where God had already determined that there would be a divine makeover.

Even before he made the world, God loved us and chose us in Christ to be holy and without fault in his eyes. God decided in advance to adopt us into his own family by bringing us to himself through Jesus Christ. This is what he wanted to do, and it gave him great pleasure. (Eph. 1:4–5)

God's plan is that all traces of sin and suffering and evil will be gone forever in a new heaven and a new earth.

What Are the New Heaven and the New Earth?

The concept of a new heaven and a new earth may be a confusing one for you. The present heaven, which we've looked at in chapter 2, is where Jesus is now. It's where we go when we die now, but that's not our permanent home. We'll be with Jesus, and as the psalmist wrote,

> No wonder my heart is glad, and I rejoice.
>> My body rests in safety.
> For you will not leave my soul among the dead
>> or allow your holy one to rot in the grave.
> You will show me the way of life,
>> granting me the joy of your presence
>> and the pleasures of living with you forever. (Ps. 16:9–11)

For those who have died before Christ's return, there will be joy and peace, but they will still be waiting to eventually return with Christ when the end-time events have taken place, and then live eternally with him in the new heaven and new earth. God will come down to be with us.

The phrase "new heaven and a new earth" occurs four times in the Bible:

Look! I am creating new heavens and a new earth, and no one will even think about the old ones anymore. (Isa. 65:17)

As surely as my new heavens and earth will remain, so will you always be my people, with a name that will never disappear. (Isa. 66:22)

But we are looking forward to the new heavens and new earth he has promised, a world filled with God's righteousness. (2 Pet. 3:13)

Then I saw a new heaven and a new earth, for the old heaven and the old earth had disappeared. And the sea was also gone. (Rev. 21:1)

In chapter 2 we looked at the three heavens that exist at the moment. The first heaven is the earth's atmosphere, where the birds and airplanes fly. The second heaven is space, where all the planets, galaxies, and stars exist. The third heaven is where Jesus and the Father are now. It's where the angels are, where they are worshiping right now. It's where you and I go the moment we die. But that is not the permanent, eternal place where we will live. As the passage in Revelation 21 shows us, our final resting place is not *up*, it's when God brings a new heaven and a new earth *down*.

But when will this take place?

What Has to Happen First Before the New Heaven and New Earth?

There are many wonderful eschatological books (books on Bible prophecy or things to come) written very specifically on the events of the end times, and it's not my intent to attempt to cover those in this book. I simply want to provide an understanding of when things will happen and when the new heaven and new earth will appear. Depending on denomination or personal study, there are differing opinions as to the order of certain end-time events. But one thing that every believer can agree on is this: Jesus has promised to return, and he will stand on the Mount of Olives, just as his disciples saw him ascend.

> **Jesus is coming back and he's coming back for you.**

> "Men of Galilee," they said, "why are you standing here staring into heaven? Jesus has been taken from you into heaven, but someday he will return from heaven in the same way you saw him go!" (Acts 1:11)

Before we dive deeper into the timing and differing opinions on when these events will take place, let me remind you of one thing you can stake your life on: Jesus is coming back and he's coming back for you.

Debate exists as to:

1. Whether the church will be "caught up" to meet Christ, and when.
2. Whether the church will still be on the earth during the seven years of the tribulation (Rev. 7:14).
3. When the second coming of Christ will be.

1. Those who believe that the church will be raptured (the word *rapture* means "caught up") before the tribulation are called pre-tribulationalists. That belief is based at least partly on this passage from Paul's letter to the church in Thessalonica.

> We tell you this directly from the Lord: We who are still living when the Lord returns will not meet him ahead of those who have died. For the Lord himself will come down from heaven with a commanding shout, with the voice of the archangel, and with the trumpet call of God. First, the believers who have died will rise from their graves. Then, together with them, we who are still alive and remain on the earth will be caught up in the clouds to meet the Lord in the air. Then we will be with the Lord forever. (1 Thess. 4:15–17)

For the rapture to happen, nothing else needs to occur. It is imminent. Christ could come at any minute and take the church out of the world and then the seven years of tribulation begin.

2. Mid-tribulationalists believe that the church will still be on earth for the first three and a half years of the tribulation and then raptured before the worst of the devastation and sorrow, the great tribulation. The passages supporting this position are slightly harder to understand. For example,

He will defy the Most High and oppress the holy people of the Most High. He will try to change their sacred festivals and laws, and they will be placed under his control for a time, times, and half a time. (Dan. 7:25)

Those who know how to interpret biblical numerology in the Hebrew text say that "a time, times, and half a time" signifies three and a half years. So they believe that the church will remain on the earth for three and a half years and then be raptured.

3. Those who hold a post-tribulation position believe that the rapture or the church being "taken up" to meet Christ and the second coming of Christ are one and the same event.

And then at last, the sign that the Son of Man is coming will appear in the heavens, and there will be deep mourning among all the peoples of the earth. And they will see the Son of Man coming on the clouds of heaven with power and great glory. And he will send out his angels with the mighty blast of a trumpet, and they will gather his chosen ones from all over the world—from the farthest ends of the earth and heaven. (Matt. 24:30–31)

Many godly men and women who love Jesus and long for his coming hold differing views and can support those views with Scripture. Honestly, what really matters is that you know Jesus, and whether you are taken up in the rapture or meet Christ at his second coming will have no impact eternally. Christ himself said that he did not know the hour of his appearance, only the Father knows that.

Heaven and earth will disappear, but my words will never disappear. However, no one knows the day or hour when these things will happen, not even the angels in heaven or the Son himself. Only the Father knows. (Matt. 24:35–36)

What we do know is that before the new heaven and new earth appear a great battle must take place. It's called the battle of Armageddon or the last battle.

Armageddon—The Last Battle

The word *Armageddon* is from the Hebrew for "Mount of Megiddo." This site, a literal place southeast of Mount Carmel, is a very famous area in Scripture. In the book of Joshua, Megiddo is listed among the towns taken by Israel when they came to the promised land (Josh. 12:21). It's also the place where King Saul died. To call Armageddon a battle doesn't come close to what will happen. This will be a war such as the world has never seen. Revelation 16 gives us a glimpse as to what this battle will look like as the antichrist gathers all his followers and demons to face the risen Christ.

In his second letter to the church in Thessalonica, Paul writes about events that must take place before the second coming of Christ and warns about the antichrist or the one he refers to as "the man of lawlessness."

> Don't be fooled by what they say. For that day will not come until there is a great rebellion against God and the man of lawlessness is revealed— the one who brings destruction. He will exalt himself and defy everything that people call god and every object of worship. He will even sit in the temple of God, claiming that he himself is God. (2 Thess. 2:3–4)

This battle will be like nothing ever seen on earth, not simply because of the engagement of all the evil forces from the four corners of the earth that have set themselves up against God Almighty, but the ease with which Christ will destroy them all.

> Then I saw the beast and the kings of the world and their armies gathered together to fight against the one sitting on the horse and his

army. And the beast was captured, and with him the false prophet who did mighty miracles on behalf of the beast—miracles that deceived all who had accepted the mark of the beast and who worshiped his statue. Both the beast and his false prophet were thrown alive into the fiery lake of burning sulfur. Their entire army was killed by the sharp sword that came from the mouth of the one riding the white horse. (Rev. 19:19–21)

Notice one thing about that last sentence. Christ, the One on the white horse, wasn't carrying a sword in his hand. He destroyed them all with what came from his mouth. A word. With one word from his mouth.

> **Christ, the Second Adam, will reverse the curse and redeem God's plan.**

The same Jesus Christ, who created all things that were made by a word from his mouth, will destroy all that is evil and an abomination with a simple word from his mouth. Christ, the Second Adam, will reverse the curse and redeem God's plan. The promise was there in Genesis 3.

And I will cause hostility between you and the woman, and between your offspring and her offspring. He will strike your head, and you will strike his heel. (Gen. 3:15)

This verse is often referred to as the "protoevangelium," meaning the first gospel. What it means is that yes, Satan will bruise Christ, the seed of Eve, on the cross, but finally Christ will crush his head and defeat him forever.

The Millennium

Then together we will rule with Christ for a thousand years, called the *millennium*. The millennium will be a thousand-year period of peace and plenty as Satan has been bound with chains.

The angel threw him into the bottomless pit, which he then shut and locked so Satan could not deceive the nations anymore until the thousand years were finished. (Rev. 20:3)

But at the end of the thousand years, Satan is released. Why? No parole, no ankle monitor, no limits put on what he can or can't do, he will just be let go. It certainly isn't to see if he will repent; he is evil to his core. I believe it is for those who are still on the earth, who have not died yet, to turn to God. The final proof of the love and mercy of God. But as we saw with Adam and Eve, a perfect environment does not guarantee a perfect relationship with God.

The Great White Throne Judgment

Then will come the Great White Throne Judgment for all who have refused the mercy of God and the sacrifice of Christ. Honestly, this is the hardest thing for me to write about. Yet knowing that such a day is coming is one of the reasons that I wrote this book. I know that it is the heart of God that no one—no one—should be lost.

The Lord isn't really being slow about his promise, as some people think. No, he is being patient for your sake. He does not want anyone to be destroyed, but wants everyone to repent. (2 Pet. 3:9)

That's why Jesus came. That's why he died in our place. But for those who resolutely refuse his grace and mercy, they get to make that choice.

And I saw a great white throne and the one sitting on it. The earth and sky fled from his presence, but they found no place to hide. I saw the dead, both great and small, standing before God's throne. And the books were opened, including the Book of Life. And the dead were judged according to what they had done, as recorded in the books. The sea gave up its dead, and death and the grave gave up their dead. And all were judged according to their deeds. Then death and the grave were thrown into the lake of fire. This lake of fire is the second death. And anyone whose name was not found recorded in the Book of Life was thrown into the lake of fire. (Rev. 20:11–15)

God is not an evil dictator who demands that we fall in line. He is a loving yet holy Father who longs for relationship. If you have been toying with making a decision to follow Christ, I urge you in Jesus's name to come home. Scripture tells us that "everyone who calls on the name of the LORD will be saved" (Rom. 10:13).

At the end of the Great White Throne Judgment, Satan will be cast into the lake of fire forever and evil will be gone (see Rev. 20:10). We will live eternally with Jesus in a new heaven and a new earth.

We will worship the same Jesus who walked the dusty streets of Jerusalem and a different Jesus, glorified forever. We will see the nail-scarred hands and feet and yet the majesty of the One who rose from the dead.

This paradox of "the same Jesus and also a different Jesus" is precisely what John was trying to communicate about the "new heavens and earth" in the book of Revelation. He was convinced that the future of the universe walked out of the tomb on Easter morning, simultaneously the same and different. What was true of the risen Jesus is what will be true for all creation when heaven and earth completely reunite.[1]

What Will This New Heaven and New Earth Look Like?

The description that is given in Revelation 21 is staggeringly beautiful. Let's look at the picture that was given to John. It's hard to take in. He used words that were available to him to describe the indescribable.

So he took me in the Spirit to a great, high mountain, and he showed me the holy city, Jerusalem, descending out of heaven from God. It shone with the glory of God and sparkled like a precious stone—like jasper as clear as crystal. The city wall was broad and high, with twelve gates guarded by twelve angels. And the names of the twelve tribes of Israel were written on the gates. There were three gates on each side—east, north, south, and west. The wall of the city had twelve foundation stones, and on them were written the names of the twelve apostles of the Lamb.

The angel who talked to me held in his hand a gold measuring stick to measure the city, its gates, and its wall. When he measured it, he found it was a square, as wide as it was long. In fact, its length and width and height were each 1,400 miles. Then he measured the walls and found them to be 216 feet thick (according to the human standard used by the angel).

The wall was made of jasper, and the city was pure gold, as clear as glass. The wall of the city was built on foundation stones inlaid with twelve precious stones: the first was jasper, the second sapphire, the third agate, the fourth emerald, the fifth onyx, the sixth carnelian, the seventh chrysolite, the eighth beryl, the ninth topaz, the tenth chrysoprase, the eleventh jacinth, the twelfth amethyst.

The twelve gates were made of pearls—each gate from a single pearl! And the main street was pure gold, as clear as glass. (Rev. 21:10–21)

It's hard to picture. What we do know is that it is unlike anything we've ever seen before. The holy city sparkled with gold and precious gems, and John describes Christ, the One sitting on the throne, as being brilliant as jasper and carnelian. That's how John first saw him.

And instantly I was in the Spirit, and I saw a throne in heaven and someone sitting on it. The one sitting on the throne was as brilliant as gemstones—like jasper and carnelian. And the glow of an emerald circled his throne like a rainbow. (Rev. 4:2–3)

I love the description of the twelve gates, each made of a single pearl. When you think of how pearls are made on earth, each one is a triumph over tribulation. As the grains of sand irritate the flesh inside the oyster, it covers the grain over and over with saliva and calcium until a perfect pearl is formed. In heaven, we will no longer need to triumph over tribulation because Christ has already done that forever.

> **In heaven, we will no longer need to triumph over tribulation because Christ has already done that forever.**

The next few verses give us a glimpse into what the new city, the new Jerusalem, will be like. There will be no temple in the city. There will be no need of a temple because God himself will be there with us. He will be the temple. There will be no need of light, of the sun or the moon, because the glory of God will shine and the Lamb is the city's light.

> I saw no temple in the city, for the Lord God Almighty and the Lamb are its temple. And the city has no need of sun or moon, for the glory of God illuminates the city, and the Lamb is its light. The nations will walk in its light, and the kings of the world will enter the city in all their glory. Its gates will never be closed at the end of day because there is no night there. And all the nations will bring their glory and honor into the city. Nothing evil will be allowed to enter, nor anyone who practices shameful idolatry and dishonesty— but only those whose names are written in the Lamb's Book of Life. (Rev. 21:22–27)

We will be able to come into the city and worship God in all his glory. We will see Jesus in his beauty, still bearing the scars of crucifixion he bore for us. It will be perpetual day, but we will never get tired and there will be fresh beauty everywhere. My friend Anne Graham Lotz paints a beautiful picture for us.

[God] created all the earthly beauty we have grown to love . . . the majestic snowcapped peaks of the Alps, the rushing mountain streams, the brilliantly colored fall leaves, the carpets of wildflowers, the glistening fin of a fish as it leaps out of a sparkling sea, the graceful gliding of a swan across the lake, the lilting notes of the canary's song, the whir of a hummingbird's wings, the shimmer of the dew on the grass in early morning. . . . This is the same Creator who has prepared our heavenly home for us! If God could make the heavens and earth as beautiful as we think they are today—which includes thousands of years of wear and tear, corruption and pollution, sin and selfishness—can you imagine what the new heaven and the new earth will look like? It will be much more glorious than any eyes have seen, any ears have heard, or any minds have ever conceived.[2]

Our New Lives on a New Earth

In the new heaven and new earth, we will finally experience what Adam and Eve did before the fall. They had the beauty and joy of walking with God in the cool of the day. Now, with Eden restored, God himself is coming down to live with us.

I have a confession to make. I always saw the new heaven and new earth as just what we read about in Revelation 21. I didn't understand that what is described there is the new Jerusalem, the new holy city. We will also have a brand-new heaven and earth to explore eternally.

Do you love the mountains? They'll be there.

Are you an ocean guy? Even though Revelation 21:1 says that the sea will be gone, it doesn't mean that there won't be water in plenty on the new earth.

Did you dream of being an astronaut as a child? Perhaps you'll get to do that then. Do you compose music? Can't wait to hear your new pieces. Are you an artist? You'll be able to paint with colors you've never seen before.

It's life as we've never even had the ability to imagine. I love the picture Randy Alcorn paints.

> And that's Immanuel. Remember that name of Jesus? *God With Us.* So ultimately the eternal heaven is not us going up to live with God in *His* place; it's God coming down to live with us in *our* place, and it's the resurrected Christ, the King of humanity, the King of kings, ruling over the new earth. And under Him, His kings and queens. You know, some who have been faithful in this much, ruling over five cities and some ruling over ten cities and dwelling together and celebrating on that new earth. His servants will serve Him.[3]

We'll know each other; we'll be in the peak of life. No more depression or anxiety. No fear or anger. Just you, a perfect you. Alcorn goes on to say:

> But my point is, I'd be depressed if I thought that I had passed my peak. Well, here's the thing. Not only have I not passed my peak, I have never seen my peak. My peak will not come until the resurrection, and I will never be less than at my peak.[4]

Then There Was Rest

When God created the heavens and the earth that we read about in Genesis, there were six days of magnificent, unprecedented work, and then there was rest. We will have the joy of working but without the frustration and exhaustion that our lives so often face each day. That was God's original plan for Adam, that he would work the land and cultivate great beauty. We will work in ways we've never imagined, perfectly suited to who we are and to our gifts and talents.

We will rest. What a beautiful thought. Our days will be filled with the most fulfilling work we've ever known and then the joy of rest. I imagine picnics by a river in fields of the greenest grass I've ever seen. I think of watching animals playing together, tumbling over one another, and then resting in a heap. I think of popping in to see friends, lavish meals around an open fire, and conversations like we've never known before. This is not wishful thinking. This is our solid hope, and so we keep walking. We keep taking the next step even as we long for a glimpse of the shore.

When You Are Weary

I know in my own life that it's easy to get discouraged and lose focus on our eternal home. As I've been writing this book it has become so much clearer to me that God has had a good plan all along. At times it's hard to see, as our lives can get a little foggy. It can happen to us all.

In 1952, young Florence Chadwick stepped into the waters of the Pacific Ocean off Catalina Island, determined to swim to the shore of mainland California. She had already been the first woman to swim the English Channel both ways. The weather was foggy and chilly; she could hardly see the boats accompanying her. Still, she swam for 15 hours. When she begged to be taken out of the water along the way, her mother, in a boat alongside, told her she was close and that she could make it. Finally, physically and emotionally exhausted, she stopped swimming and was pulled out. It wasn't until she was on the boat that she discovered the shore was less than half a mile away. At a news conference the next days she said, "All I could see was the fog . . . I think if I could have seen the shore, I would have made it."[5]

We all need a glimpse of the shore.

I wonder how often you get tired swimming *home* as a believer. It feels as if that's all you've done for so long, and you're worn out. You've faithfully served, you've studied your Bible, you've helped others, and quite honestly, you are just worn out. That's why I think we need a little glimpse of the shores of home and of Jesus. He will no longer be a fragile baby, wrapped in swaddling clothes; he will be seen as he is, King of Kings and Lord of Lords.

I think C. S. Lewis painted a perfect picture as he brought his Chronicles of Narnia series to a close in *The Last Battle*. As Queen Lucy, King Edmund, and King Peter find themselves in the new heaven and new earth, they see their parents and their old friend Mr. Tumnus. Finally, they see Aslan himself. It seems only right and wise that Lewis ends this final story without being able to put into words the indescribable beauty of what is waiting for us on the shores of home. That would require language that we've not learned yet, colors we've never seen, music that is breathtakingly alive. He writes that rather than the end of all the stories it's really just the beginning. Like the tuning up of the orchestra before the curtains open and the play begins.

This is our certain future. Every year, every month, every day, every single moment greater than our wildest imaginings.

Father God,
I can only begin to imagine what my life will be like in the new heaven and the new earth when you come down to us, when you make your home with us. Help me to keep my eyes fixed on you as I journey home.
Amen.

What I Know about Heaven

I will live with Jesus forever in a new heaven and a new earth, fully alive, fully awake, fully loved. Finally home.

9

HOW DOES HEAVEN CHANGE THE WAY WE LIVE TODAY?

Think about the things of heaven, not the things of earth. For you died to this life, and your real life is hidden with Christ in God. And when Christ, who is your life, is revealed to the whole world, you will share in all his glory.

Colossians 3:2–4

If you had to give an elevator pitch about who you are as a person, what would you say? How would you define and summarize your life? Depending on who we're talking to, we often identify ourselves by our relationships—who we're married to or who our parents or children are.

This is Sam's wife, Elaine.

Have you met Tony? He's Ken's son.

At other times we identify ourselves by our job or who we work for.

I'm the vice president of the largest bank in town.

I'm a stay-at-home mom.

In a culture that's becoming increasingly divided, we might identify ourselves by our political affiliation or religious beliefs.

But what if you had to go deeper? What if rather than who you're related to, where you work, or what your public stance is on issues, it was a core belief about yourself that impacts everything you do, how you see yourself, and how you serve Christ? That can be more challenging to identify.

For over thirty years I've had an internal identity statement that was powerful to me. I've written about it in previous books. It was how I saw myself for almost all of those years, and that was a good thing. It brought me comfort and hope, a feeling of safety and belonging. Recently, that is changing. I'm changing. The more I'm thinking about the things of heaven, the more I'm changing here on earth. Perhaps I should start with where that internal identity came from and why for so many years I saw myself simply as a *bummer lamb*.

When Your Life Falls Apart

I've mentioned in a previous chapter that after my father's death by suicide when I was five, I became very careful. Life no longer was safe or kind. I believed that at some core level I was broken. Relationships seemed fragile and conditional to me.

Because I felt that I was in some way responsible for my father's death, I carried so much guilt and shame. When you combine that kind of internal brokenness with a strong belief in God, as Father, you can end up with a very distorted faith. If you believe that your earthly father's love for you was removed for reasons that are hard to understand as a child, it's a short step to conclude that God's love is based on your performance as well. All through my late teens and twenties and into my thirties I worked like a crazy person trying to prove to God that I was worth loving. Inside I was pretty miserable or numb most of the time, but I had made peace with that. That was my normal. I believed that heaven was where you go to collapse when you've finally crossed the finishing line. All I had to do was keep going, keep my face to the wind, and keep walking, which worked until it didn't anymore.

Earlier I shared some of the details of when my life fell apart and I ended up in a psychiatric hospital. It was what I'd always been afraid of, tangible proof of how broken I was. I didn't realize in those first days in the hospital how that experience would change how I saw my life. It started with a strange encounter.

For the first couple of days, I was placed on suicide watch. Someone would check on me every fifteen minutes during the night as I sat on the floor in the corner of my room, unable to sleep. I was in such a dark place that I didn't pay any attention to who was coming into my room until the person who came in at three o'clock in the morning walked over and handed something to me. It was something you would give a child. It was a small stuffed lamb. He turned to leave my room but paused at the door and said one thing, "Sheila, the Shepherd knows where to find you."

The Shepherd knows where to find you.

Eight words, but they were like a lighthouse in a storm. I felt like such a failure, a disappointment, but those words told me that God was not finished with me. I believe my visitor was an angel. I was there for a month and never saw him again. As I held that little lamb, it reminded me of an interesting thing that happens in nature that spoke so profoundly to me.

Every now and then a ewe will give birth to a lamb and immediately reject it. Those lambs are called *bummer lambs*. The shepherd has to intervene or the lamb will die, not of hunger but of a broken spirit. He will take that little one into his home, feed it with a bottle, and keep it warm. When he holds the lamb close to his heart, the lamb becomes familiar with his voice, so much so that when the lamb is strong enough to be returned to the flock, it will always run to the shepherd ahead of the rest of the flock when he appears. That picture became so vivid for me. Christ identified himself as the Good Shepherd.

> The sheep recognize his voice and come to him. He calls his own sheep by name and leads them out. After he has gathered his own flock, he walks ahead of them, and they follow him because they know his voice. (John 10:3–4)

The shepherd doesn't love the bummer lambs more than the rest of his flock, but they have a relationship. The shepherd held them when they were broken. I know that Christ, the Good Shepherd, doesn't love his *bummer lambs* more than the rest of his people; it's just that we finally understood that at our worst, our most broken, we have been held, and we know his voice. We don't hope that we are loved; we know that we are loved. So that became my identity, and it gave me so much comfort and hope.

From Lambs to Lions

Since I began studying to write this book, so much is changing in me. I always had the hope of heaven, but I honestly didn't understand what I was hoping for, what that hope would look like. Everything is changing for me now. When I take a walk in the morning, I lift my eyes toward heaven and have a new understanding that on my best days and worst days my eternal future is secure. I'm not struggling to get through this life. I'm living in the power of the risen Christ. In his strength,

> **In his strength, lambs become lions.**

lambs become lions. That's what I long for in your life as well. I'm asking the Holy Spirit to help you see that no matter what your life might look like at the moment, the joys and sadness, the wins and losses, the surprises and disappointments, because of Jesus, we win! We are part of heaven's royal family, and no one can take that away from us. So, yes, I still love the tender picture of the bummer lamb, but my new internal identity based on the finished work of Christ looks a little different. The origin of this phrase is unknown, but it's used as a line in Ridley Scott's movie *Robin Hood*:

Rise and rise again until lambs become lions.[1]

When we begin to grasp who we are and whose we are, it changes everything. In this chapter, I want us to focus on a few things we know for sure about heaven that impact how we live here and now on earth. When we can grasp these truths, although we will fall at times, we will be given the strength to rise and rise again. Then we'll unpack a parable that Jesus told that directly speaks to how you and I should live today and all of our tomorrows.

No More Death

As I was writing this chapter, my phone buzzed with a breaking news story about a bus crash in Italy that killed at least twenty-one people. Twenty-one souls boarded that bus, tourists who were heading to a campsite just outside Vienna. No one had any idea that the bus would fail to make a turn and plunge over a bridge and catch fire. Two children were among the dead. My heart ached as I read the story. Whether it's the horror of what happened on 9/11 or a lone

> **The life-changing news about death is that because of Jesus, it has a limited shelf life. Death has an expiration date.**

crash on a local highway, we internally rebel and cry out at the reality of death. The life-changing news about death is that because of Jesus, it has a limited shelf life. Death has an expiration date.

> He will swallow up death forever! The Sovereign LORD will wipe away all tears. (Isa. 25:8)

Paul wrote these words of encouragement to the church in Corinth:

> Then, when our dying bodies have been transformed into bodies that will never die, this Scripture will be fulfilled:
> "Death is swallowed up in victory.
> O death, where is your victory?
> O death, where is your sting?"
> For sin is the sting that results in death, and the law gives sin its power. But thank God! He gives us victory over sin and death through our Lord Jesus Christ.
> So, my dear brothers and sisters, be strong and immovable. Always work enthusiastically for the Lord, for you know that nothing you do for the Lord is ever useless. (1 Cor. 15:54–58)

I love the way Paul connects the reality that death is coming to an end to a rallying cry for us to live differently now. That is the hope that gives us the strength to rise and rise again. We no longer have to be afraid of death. We can fully engage in living.

No More Grief

One of my best friends lost her mom a few weeks ago. I talk to her every day as she grieves the loss of the one who gave her life and love, direction and comfort. Most of the time I just listen as she remembers. Having buried my mum, I remember the pain. I don't think you are ever prepared to say goodbye to your mom or dad. Grief seems to come in waves. You feel as if the worst is over and then something triggers a memory or a familiar scent can bring a fresh wave that you feel might take you under.

We all grieve differently over different things that happen in our lives. Last year we had to have our little bichon frise, Tink, put to sleep. She was sixteen years old, and when it was clear that she was suffering, it was the only thing to do. But it has been hard grieving the loss of this little dog. She always slept in our bed, right between our heads. She was like a child to us. The promise of heaven is that all grief will be gone forever.

> He will wipe every tear from their eyes. There will be no more death or mourning or crying or pain, for the old order of things has passed away. (Rev. 21:4 NIV)

In his commentary on the book of Revelation, Albert Barnes says this:

> How innumerable are the sources of sorrow here; how constant is it on the earth! Since the fall of man there has not been a day, an hour, a moment, in which this has not been a sorrowful world; there has not been a nation, a tribe, a city or a village nay, not a family, where there has not been grief. There has been no individual who has been always perfectly happy. No one rises in the morning with any certainty that he may not end the day in grief; no one lies down at night with any assurance that it may not be a night of sorrow. How different would this world be if it were announced that henceforward there would be no sorrow! How different, therefore, will heaven be when we shall have the assurance that henceforward grief shall be at an end.[2]

No more! All grief, sorrow, regret, second-guessing, gone forever. This is not wishful thinking; this is a promise from God himself.

No Longer Will There Be a Curse

I will never forget the first time I saw my son. For nine months I knew that he was my son, but my understanding of all that meant was limited. As the weeks passed and I felt those first flutters of life, my love grew and grew. At our ultrasound as we listened to his heartbeat and saw the outline of his little body, I was overwhelmed. But nothing prepared me for that moment when the nurse placed him in my arms and I was able to see him face-to-face. He looked quite cross, and I commented to Barry that he had a tan. (I later discovered that it was jaundice, not the result of living in California.) He's twenty-seven now, and my heart still swells with love when he FaceTimes with Barry and me.

There is something wonderful about being face-to-face with someone you love. Can you even begin to imagine what that will be like when we see Jesus face-to-face? At the conclusion of the Revelation, the apostle John writes about the freedom and joy in the new Eden.

No longer will there be a curse upon anything. For the throne of God and of the Lamb will be there, and his servants will worship him. And they will see his face, and his name will be written on their foreheads. (Rev. 22:3–4)

Again John writes,

Dear friends, we are already God's children, but he has not yet shown us what we will be like when Christ appears. But we do know that we will be like him, for we will see him as he really is. (1 John 3:2)

To be with Jesus, to see him as he is, all the time, is beyond my ability to fathom. If you're like me, there are days when you feel God's presence so close, but there are also days when he seems so far away. There are days when it's easy to believe that God is good and merciful and loving, but I know there can be days when that's harder. When you've prayed and prayed for the healing of a loved one or you're doing all you can to provide for your family, but it feels as if your prayers are not being heard, it's easy to struggle with what you don't understand.

> **When God himself comes down to earth to live with us, to be with us, we will never have a moment of doubt or pain again.**

Those days are coming to an end. When we see Jesus face-to-face, when God himself comes down to earth to live with us, to be with us, we will never have a moment of doubt or pain again.

No More Hurt

One of the things I'm most looking forward to in heaven is the reality that all of our relationships will be perfect. There will be no more hurt or misunderstandings or moments when we feel left out or when we say the wrong thing. I've always struggled a bit with relationships. Because I felt so broken for so many years, that brought with it its own tasting menu.

I'm sure they would rather I hadn't come.
I'm sure they don't like me.
I'm not enough.
I'm too broken.
I wish I hadn't said that.
She is much more capable than me.

The list could go on, but I'm sure you get the idea. You may have your own list. We all feel like we're not quite enough in one way or another. Even those among us who seem the most confident, bordering on arrogant, are often disguising feelings of "not-enoughness." The best marriages, the closest friendships can be wounded by

You have all the grace you need. careless words. In a world where we've often exchanged talking to one another for texting, we don't always communicate as clearly as we'd intended to. In the new heaven and new earth, that will be gone forever. We will see one another as we are, we will know one another, we will hear one another clearly, and we will love one another perfectly.

Until then, we hold on to who Jesus says we are:

1. You are chosen.
    "We know, dear brothers and sisters, that God loves you and has chosen you to be his own people" (1 Thess. 1:4).
2. You are a new creation.
    "This means that anyone who belongs to Christ has become a new person. The old life is gone; a new life has begun!" (2 Cor. 5:17).
3. You are forgiven.
    "He is so rich in kindness and grace that he purchased our freedom with the blood of his Son and forgave our sins" (Eph. 1:7).
4. You are blessed.
    "So all who put their faith in Christ share the same blessing Abraham received because of his faith" (Gal. 3:9).
5. You have been set free.
    "And you will know the truth, and the truth will set you free" (John 8:32).
6. You can know his peace.
    "Don't worry about anything; instead, pray about everything. Tell God what you need, and thank him for all he has done. Then you will experience God's peace, which exceeds anything we can understand. His peace will guard your hearts and minds as you live in Christ Jesus" (Phil. 4:6–7).

7. You are loved.

"See how very much our Father loves us, for he calls us his children, and that is what we are!" (1 John 3:1).

8. You are strong in the Lord.

"A final word: Be strong in the Lord and in his mighty power" (Eph. 6:10).

9. You are not condemned.

"So now there is no condemnation for those who belong to Christ Jesus" (Rom. 8:1).

10. You have all the grace you need.

"[The Lord said,] 'My grace is all you need. My power works best in weakness.' So now I am glad to boast about my weaknesses, so that the power of Christ can work through me" (2 Cor. 12:9).

No More Unmet Needs

I struggle with the unfairness in this world. I would love this world to be fair and it's not. I didn't get to choose what family I was born into. Although the death of my father was a tragedy that left its mark on me, I was raised by a godly mother who loved me. I was able, through a scholarship, to get a full ride to seminary and make choices in my life to follow the path I believed God had called me to. But I've spent a lot of time over the years in Africa where mothers care for children who are born into abject poverty, where there is no access to nutritional food and no clean water. I've worked for years in Thailand and Cambodia where girls as young as ten and eleven are trafficked for sex. This world is not fair. I'm sure you see it in your own circles too, things that make you shake your head and wonder when the world became this crazy. The day is coming when all of that will be gone. The friend you have who seems to be facing one disaster after another. The family that has way more than their share of the hard things in life. Perhaps you are that one. You ask yourself, "What did I do wrong, Lord? I've done all I know to do to honor you and yet it's just one slammed door after another." Hold on, my friend. Those days are numbered. Because we know without a shadow of a doubt that this is true, because of Jesus, we can rise and rise again.

> They will never again be hungry or thirsty;
> they will never be scorched by the heat of the sun.
> For the Lamb on the throne
> will be their Shepherd.
> He will lead them to springs of life-giving water.
> And God will wipe every tear from their eyes. (Rev. 7:16–17)

No More Sin

Do you ever find yourself saying, "I can't believe I did that again." It's one of the hallmarks of life on this earth that we revisit the very places we said we'd never stop by again. The apostle Paul wrote about it in one of the most relatable passages in his letter to the church in Rome.

> I have discovered this principle of life—that when I want to do what is right, I inevitably do what is wrong. I love God's law with all my heart. But there is another power within me that is at war with my mind. This power makes me a slave to the sin that is still within me. Oh, what a miserable person I am! Who will free me from this life that is dominated by sin and death? (Rom. 7:21–24)

Thankfully, Paul knew the answer.

> Thank God! The answer is in Jesus Christ our Lord. (v. 25)

The weariness and dreariness of this life will be no more. I love the way Mark Hitchcock writes about life in our forever home.

Think about it. We will never sin, never make mistakes, never need to confess, never have to repair or replace things (no leaky faucets, no changing lightbulbs, no car repairs). We will never have to help others, defend ourselves, apologize, experience guilt, battle with Satan or demons, share the gospel of Jesus Christ, or experience healing, rehabilitation, loneliness, depression, or fatigue.[3]

Done. Over. Finished. Home free.

How Should We Then Live?

Knowing all of this, understanding that death and sorrow will be gone forever, knowing that our relationships will be perfect, that all the tedious work and the questions that have weighed us down for so long will be banished, how should that impact the way we live today? Do we simply hold on and wait for this life to be over, for Jesus to come and get us out of here, or is there another way to live? I am so glad you asked! Jesus tells two stories in Matthew's Gospel that speak directly to that question. The stories don't just speak to it, they shine the brightest light on it. They show us that the choices we make today and tomorrow will impact all our eternal todays and tomorrows.

If you read chapters 24 and 25 of Matthew's Gospel, you can feel the clock ticking down. The final grains of sand are running out on Christ's life on earth. He is talking to his closest friends about the events that will happen in the future, and they want to know when the events he is speaking about will happen.

> Later, Jesus sat on the Mount of Olives. His disciples came to him privately and said, "Tell us, when will all this happen? What sign will signal your return and the end of the world?" (24:3)

Jesus tells them that, as no one but the Father knows the hour when he will return, they should be ready, they should be waiting, they should be expectant. Most of us find it challenging to maintain a constant expectancy when we have to wait much longer than we imagined. Whether it's waiting to hear if your child got into their school of choice or if you'll get that promotion you've been waiting for or if it's finally time to retire, we struggle with maintaining hopeful expectation as we wait.

Not so for our four-legged friends. If I'm out of town for a couple of days, Barry has learned not to tell Maggie that I'm coming home until I text him to say that I'm about ten minutes out. He learned that the hard way. A few months ago, I'd left on a Thursday and was coming home on the following Sunday, but on Saturday night he told her, "Mommy's coming home tomorrow." Maggie positioned herself by the front door and wouldn't move. He had to carry her up to bed that night, but even then she wouldn't stay in bed. She jumped off and lay by the door. The following morning, she assumed her position by the front door and sat there for four hours until I came home. If only that was my heart as I watch for Christ's return.

The first parable in Matthew 25 is about ten bridesmaids. Five had made allowance for the potential of the groom being delayed and five had not. When his return took longer than any of them anticipated, the five who had brought extra oil for their lamps were ready for the celebration and invited in. The other five were caught off guard and shut out.

So you, too, must keep watch! For you do not know the day or hour of my return. (v. 13)

In this parable Jesus is saying, be ready, be watching and waiting. But then Jesus goes on to tell a story about what we should be doing as we wait.

Again, the Kingdom of Heaven can be illustrated by the story of a man going on a long trip. He called together his servants and entrusted his money to them while he was gone. He gave five bags of silver to one, two bags of silver to another, and one bag of silver to the last—dividing it in proportion to their abilities. He then left on his trip.

The servant who received the five bags of silver began to invest the money and earned five more. The servant with two bags of silver also went to work and earned two more. But the servant who received the one bag of silver dug a hole in the ground and hid the master's money.

After a long time their master returned from his trip and called them to give an account of how they had used his money. The servant to whom he had entrusted the five bags of silver came forward with five more and said, "Master, you gave me five bags of silver to invest, and I have earned five more."

The master was full of praise. "Well done, my good and faithful servant. You have been faithful in handling this small amount, so now I will give you many more responsibilities. Let's celebrate together!"

The servant who had received the two bags of silver came forward and said, "Master, you gave me two bags of silver to invest, and I have earned two more."

The master said, "Well done, my good and faithful servant. You have been faithful in handling this small amount, so now I will give you many more responsibilities. Let's celebrate together!"

Then the servant with the one bag of silver came and said, "Master, I knew you were a harsh man, harvesting crops you didn't plant and gathering crops you didn't cultivate. I was afraid I would lose your money, so I hid it in the earth. Look, here is your money back."

But the master replied, "You wicked and lazy servant! If you knew I harvested crops I didn't plant and gathered crops I didn't cultivate, why didn't you deposit my money in the bank? At least I could have gotten some interest on it."

Then he ordered, "Take the money from this servant, and give it to the one with the ten bags of silver. To those who use well what they are given, even more will be given, and they will have an abundance. But from those who do nothing, even what little they have will be taken away. Now throw this useless servant into outer darkness, where there will be weeping and gnashing of teeth." (vv. 14–30)

This parable is as clear as it gets. Have you ever wondered what you could be doing with your life that would please God? I know I have. Well, here Jesus tells us.

It's clear in this story that the master gives each one of his servants a different amount of money according to how he views their ability. He gives one servant five bags of silver, another two bags of silver, and, to the final servant, one bag of silver, and then he leaves on his trip. While he's gone, the one with five bags of silver invests it wisely and doubles the money entrusted to him, as does the servant with two bags. The servant with one bag, however, buries his in his backyard. He doesn't do anything bad or illegal with the money. He just does nothing. When the master returns from his trip, the servant who had been given five bags presents ten bags to his master.

> The master was full of praise. "Well done, my good and faithful servant. You have been faithful in handling this small amount, so now I will give you many more responsibilities. Let's celebrate together!" (v. 21)

The servant who had been given two bags comes forward and presents four bags to his master. I find it interesting that the master says exactly the same to him as he did to the one with ten bags.

> The master said, "Well done, my good and faithful servant. You have been faithful in handling this small amount, so now I will give you many more responsibilities. Let's celebrate together!" (v. 23)

He doesn't say, "Well that's great, not as much as the first servant but not bad considering that's all I gave you to start." He is as pleased with the second servant as he was with the first. When the third servant comes forward, his approach is totally different. Rather than presenting what he has, he begins by tearing into his master, criticizing his style of leadership, and using that as an excuse for the fact that he has done nothing at all with the money he'd been given. He tells his master that he was afraid of him and so fear stopped him from doing anything at all. The master is furious with him, and what he had been given was taken away.

So, how does this story relate to us today? What was Jesus saying to his friends and to us? Let's look at the first two servants as they relate to you and me.

It's clear that some of us are more gifted than others. When you listen to a voice like Pavarotti, gaze at the works of Michelangelo, or marvel at the mind of a brilliant scientist or mathematician, it's clear that some people are extraordinarily gifted. In many ways, it's relative. Context is everything. We can assume that we are unusually gifted until someone else shows up on the scene. When I was sixteen years old, I saved up from my summer job and bought a guitar. I taught myself a few chords, enough to be able to play a few basic songs. I mastered "If I Could" (or "El Condor Pasa" to give its proper title) by Simon and Garfunkel and a few Christian tunes that were popular at the time. I actually went into schools and gave lunchtime concerts, until I heard someone else play the guitar and thought to myself, "Oh. That's how it's supposed to sound." I sold my guitar and studied vocals. Before I came to America, I was the top Christian recording artist in the United Kingdom (I was also one of the very few), and then I was signed to an American record label. I went from being a whale of an artist in a small pond to a minnow in a very large pond.

We all face moments like that when we realize that, yes, we have been given gifts, but they might not be as impressive as someone else's gifts. What's clear from the story that Jesus told is that how great our gifts are doesn't matter at all to God. After all, he is the one who gave them out in the first place. All that matters is what we will do with what we've been given. We live in a culture and, at times, a church that elevates giftedness. None of us can take credit for the gifts we've been given. They are just that, gifts. We are able to glorify God by what we do with them.

Will we be resentful and jealous because they are less than someone else's?

Will we try and elevate ourselves over someone else?

Will we despise what we've been given and bury it?

Or will we take every single gift that we've been given and use it for the King and his kingdom?

Think about this for a moment. What are your gifts? Where are those moments when you feel most alive? What are the things you do that you sense God's hand on? Perhaps you haven't received as much positive feedback as you'd like; no one seems to notice, but Jesus does. Jesus misses nothing. If you are in a nine-to-five job with little room given for you to shine, don't let that discourage you. When you do everything you can with everything you've been given, Jesus sees that. You may be a stay-at-home mom who feels that you are doing the same pile of laundry over and over and over. Your family might not notice everything you do, but Jesus does. You may be retired and feel as if the best part of your life is over, but as you sit and pray for your family, for the church, and for those who are hurting in the world, you are making a huge difference. When we use whatever the Master has given us, Jesus sees it all.

Rise and Rise Again

Jesus made it clear that day as he sat on the Mount of Olives and talked to his closest friends that if you and I want to live the kind of life that will bring joy and celebration when Jesus finally returns, then we need to keep watch and use everything he has deposited within us to bring him glory. That makes it sound easy, doesn't it? The truth is, it's not. We're broken, we're human, and we'll fall and fail. That's when we rest in the grace of God, take a deep breath, and rise and rise again as we watch and wait.

I love how Dr. David Jeremiah contrasts the way that Jesus first came to us, as a tiny, fragile baby, and the triumphant way in which he will return.

> He entered the world the first time, in swaddling clothes;
> He will reign the second time in majestic purple.
>
> He came the first time as a weary traveler;
> He will return the second time as the untiring God.
>
> Once when He came, He had nowhere to lay His head;
> When He comes back, He will be revealed as the heir of all things.
>
> Once He was rejected by tiny Israel;
> When He returns, He will be accepted by every single nation.
>
> Once He was a lowly Savior, acquainted with grief;
> Then He will be the mighty God, anointed with the oil of gladness.
>
> Once He was smitten with a reed;
> Then He will rule the nations with a rod of iron.
>
> Once wicked soldiers bowed the knee in mockery;
> Then every knee will bow and every tongue confess that He is Lord.
>
> Once He received a crown of thorns;
> Then He will receive a crown of gold.
>
> Once He delivered up His Spirit in death;
> Then He will be alive forevermore.

Once He was laid in a tomb;
Then He will sit on a throne.[4]

How we live on this earth matters. Understanding who we are matters. Anticipating how we will live eternally matters. Even the

> **Heaven changes everything. So, let's rise and rise again!**

most fragile bummer lamb filled with the Spirit of the living Christ can become a lion. When we are done on this earth, we have really only begun to live. I love the way Victor Hugo, one of my favorite authors, describes that dawn.

I feel within me that future life. I am like a forest that has been razed; the new shoots are stronger and brighter. I shall most certainly rise toward the heavens the nearer my approach to the end, the plainer is the sound of immortal symphonies of worlds which invite me. For half a century I have been translating my thoughts into prose and verse: history, drama, philosophy, romance, tradition, satire, ode, and song; all of these I have tried. But I feel I haven't given utterance to the thousandth part of what lies within me. When I go to the grave I can say, as others have said, "My day's work is done." But I cannot say, "My life is done." My work will recommence the next morning. The tomb is not a blind alley; it is a thoroughfare. It closes upon the twilight but opens upon the dawn.[5]

Until we have finally reached our eternal home, we haven't even begun to really live. And that is why heaven changes everything. So, let's rise and rise again!

Father God,
As I wait expectantly for Christ, the spotless Lamb, to return in triumph, give me the grace to use every gift you have placed in me no matter how small it seems to bring glory to your name.
Amen.

What I Know about Heaven

My eternal identity is secure with Christ in heaven, and how I choose to live each day on earth now will add to the celebration in heaven when I am finally home.

CONCLUSION

THE HOPE OF HEAVEN

At the beginning of every year, I put my life back on the table and ask God how he would like me to serve him in the weeks and months ahead. I never want to assume that because I have been called to do something in one season that it will be the same as a new year breaks. On New Year's Eve 2021, Barry and I spent some time praying together about the year ahead. The one thing that felt clear to both of us was that change was coming. We didn't know what that would look like, but we were sure that some things were going to change. At first nothing changed, but I've learned that God's timing is often very different from mine. A whole year passed and again we stopped and put everything back on the table and waited. In the following weeks and months, a word kept growing in my heart and it was the word *hope*. Every time I opened my Bible, *hope* would be there. In texts from friends the word *hope* would be central. I was confronted by *hope* at every turn.

Halfway through 2022, Matt and Laurie Crouch invited Barry and me to join the executive staff of Trinity Broadcasting Network. We've been friends with them since Matt produced my first music video. We both love television and were grateful to accept. One of my first assignments was filming a ten-part series in Israel. It was there as I walked in the footsteps of Jesus that *hope* began to surround me. Now, clearly, as a Christian for many years, hope has always been part of my life, but this was different. This felt like heavy hope, hope with the weight of glory attached. I walked by the edge of the Sea of Galilee. I sat on the Mount of Beatitudes. I walked up the Via Dolorosa and saw the garden of Gethsemane. I knelt by the place where many believe Christ's body was laid and saw the empty tomb. I walked along the road to Emmaus and imagined what it was like that day for the two who were joined on that journey by the risen Christ (Luke 24:13–34). I saw the path that *hope* took.

> **Hope has a name, and his name is Jesus.**

Hope is an interesting word. It's just four letters but it bears a lot of weight. It can make you feel that anything is possible, it can put fresh wind in your sails, or it can crush you when it doesn't deliver on its promise. I told you that as I began to write this book I was struggling in many ways with hope. There is so much heartache all around. I see it in the lives of dear friends, in our nation, and on the international stage. This world simply doesn't work the way God originally designed it to work. We are too broken to be selfless and too polarized to see one another fully. Even in the church, we often find it easier to make assumptions and judge one another than pull each other closer to listen and learn and love. But as I began to soak myself in what God's Word says about the hope of heaven, I feel as if the Holy Spirit has washed my eyes so that I could see the bigger picture of what God has been doing all along.

I wanted to be able to have answers to the suffering and the pain in a way that made sense to me. I was looking for answers until I realized that there is only one answer: Hope has a name, and his name is Jesus.

Jesus changes everything. He came to a world where some would be born into loving families and be given every opportunity in life and some would be born into abject poverty, to cruelty and despair. He came to those the world regards as strong and gifted and to those who struggle their entire lives. He came to those granted a long life and to those whose lives are cut off before they have begun to really live. He came to you, and he came to me.

If somehow we were all asked to stand on a stage together, one thing would be immediately clear: Life is not fair. The *why* questions would be deafening. They would be deafening until we were asked to turn around and see that we are all standing at the foot of the cross, and there, as we stand gazing up, the ground is absolutely level.

The invitation is the same for everyone. Everyone must answer this question: What are you going to do with Jesus?

You might be tempted to say that the ones who have had a better life would find it easier to believe in a God of love than those who struggle. I'm not sure that is true. Sometimes an easier life can blind us to our desperate need for Christ. I have knelt with a mother beside the grave of her two-year-old child, who died because the only water she had to give him came from a contaminated hand-dug well in a remote village in Africa. She told me that without her faith she could not go on. She told me that her great comfort is that her little one is safe in heaven with Christ and one day she will be with him again.

> **The hope of heaven is there for all who will say yes!**

The hope of heaven is there for all who will say yes! We cling to our seventy or eighty years and try and wring every moment of joy and purpose out of them, but our lives here on earth are like a vapor, here then gone. Our lives with Jesus in eternity are forever.

I'm no longer fed up with this world. God has reminded me that there has always been a glorious plan in place. The scarlet thread of the grace and mercy of God began in the garden of Eden, crossed deserts and oceans and finally up to a hill called Calvary, then rose in triumph from the grave.

So now I'm looking up and I'm waiting and I'm expectant. We've not even begun to live. Hold on to Jesus. He is coming soon.

Look, I am coming soon! My reward is with me, and I will give to each person according to what they have done. I am the Alpha and the Omega, the First and the Last, the Beginning and the End. (Rev. 22:12–13 NIV)

The final words of the Bible speak of the hope and grace that will hold each one of us until he comes again.

He who testifies to these things says, "Yes, I am coming soon."
Amen! Come, Lord Jesus!
The grace of the Lord Jesus be with God's people. Amen. (Rev. 22:20–21)

The promise of eternity changes everything.

ACKNOWLEDGMENTS

First of all, thank you to the entire Baker Publishing family. President Jesse Myers, you and your team continue to uphold the rich heritage of Baker's commitment to building up the body of Christ through books. It's an honor to publish with you.

Thank you to my wonderful editor, Rebekah Von Lintel, and the entire editorial team. I'm grateful for your vision, and your hard and creative work, Rebekah, in the middle of planning a wedding!

Thank you to Eileen Hanson. I love working closely with you, and when you fly into Dallas for dinner, that's the best. You make me laugh and you make me think, and you are so good at what you do.

Thank you to the amazing Baker sales team. You have such a gift for understanding the heart of a message and championing it.

Thank you to Holly Scheevel and Olivia Peitsch. You are always looking for new ways to get the message out. I'm so grateful for you.

Thank you to Laura Powell for your caring and creative artistic direction and your endless patience with me. You are a joy to work with.

Thank you to my amazing literary agent, Shannon Marven. Shannon, you are one of the most gifted people I know. You lead with grace, compassion, and vision.

Thank you to Sydney Delahoussaye and the entire team at Dupree Miller.

Thank you to Caleb Peavy and Jessica Peavy and the staff at Unmutable. I am grateful for your creativity and the level of excellence you bring to every project.

Thank you to Matt and Laurie Crouch for your passion and vision for excellence in Christian television at Trinity Broadcasting Network. I love working side by side with you. You are family to me.

I want to thank my little dog, Maggie, for sitting patiently at my feet month after month as I wrote and for the occasional much-needed lick and the very frequent barks.

To my husband, Barry, thank you seems inadequate to express my gratitude for the amount of time and creative energy you devoted to this book. You walked and prayed through every step with me, sitting up until midnight reading chapters out loud, making countless cups of tea. I love you and thank God for you every day.

To my son, Christian. Your FaceTime calls and texts to cheer me on meant so much. I love being your mum.

Finally, to the One I will never find enough words to thank. To God my Father for loving me, to Christ my Savior for giving your life for me, and to the Holy Spirit for your comfort and guidance. I am yours forever. I am held, and one day I'll be home.

NOTES

Chapter One Is Heaven Really Real?

1. Martin Williams, "Just One in Three Scots Now Identify as a Christian," *Herald Scotland*, March 9, 2022, https://www.heraldscotland.com/news/homenews /19978556.just-one-three-scots-now-identify-christian.

2. William Barclay, *The Gospel of John*, vol. 2 (Edinburgh: St. Andrew's Press, 1975), 154.

3. Eliza E. Hewitt, "When We All Get to Heaven," 1898, Hymnary.org, https:// hymnary.org/text/sing_the_wondrous_love_of_jesus_sing_his.

Chapter Two What Is Heaven Like?

1. The Reverend Penny Jones, "Julian of Norwich: 'All Shall Be Well,'" *Anglican Focus*, May 1, 2020, https://anglicanfocus.org.au/2020/05/01/julian-of-norwich-all -shall-be-well.

2. Wikipedia, s.v. "George Sanders," last modified February 5, 2024, https://en .wikipedia.org/wiki/George_Sanders#cite_note-44.

3. Randy Alcorn, *Heaven* (Carol Stream, IL: Tyndale, 2004), 411.

Chapter Three Will Heaven Heal Our Disappointments?

1. Frederick Buechner, *The Magnificent Defeat* (United Kingdom: HarperCollins, 1985), 91.

2. The discussion that follows is based on C. S. Lewis, *Mere Christianity* (New York: Touchstone, 1996), 120–21.

Chapter Four Does Everyone Go to Heaven?

1. "What Does the Greek Word 'Tetelestai' Mean?," Bible.org, January 1, 2001, https://bible.org/question/what-does-greek-word-tetelestai-mean.

2. "Czar Nicholas Pays a Great Debt!," *Come Home: Gospel Stories*, BibleTruth, accessed September 10, 2023, https://bibletruthpublishers.com/czar-nicholas-pays -a-great-debt/come-home-gospel-stories/j-n-darby/la169641.

3. Erwin W. Lutzer, "John Harper's Last Convert," Moody Church Media, 2012, accessed September 11, 2023, https://www.moodymedia.org/articles/sharing -gift-christmas-one-minute-you-die.

Chapter Five My Dog, My Cat, and Will I Be Fat?

1. Joni Eareckson Tada, *Holiness in Hidden Places* (Nashville: J. Countryman, 1999), 133.

2. Randy Alcorn, "Will There Be Animals in Heaven?" Eternal Perspectives Ministries, February 3, 2010, https://www.epm.org/resources/2010/Feb/3/will-there -be-animals-heaven.

3. J. John, *Will I Be Fat in Heaven? and Other Curious Questions* (Rickmansworth, UK: Philo Trust, 2022), 109–10.

4. Randy Alcorn, "Suicide, Heaven, and Jesus—the Final Answer to Our Sorrow," Eternal Perspectives Ministries, October 7, 2019, https://www.epm.org/blog /2019/Oct/7/suicide-heaven-jesus-sorrow.

5. Jack Wellman, "How Old Will We Be in Heaven?" Faith in the News, accessed September 15, 2023, https://faithinthenews.com/how-old-will-we-be-in-heaven.

6. J. C. Ryle, "Home at Last!," Teaching Resources International, January 17, 2010, https://teachingresources.org/2010/01/17/home-at-last-by-j-c-ryle.

7. Billy Graham, *The Heaven Answer Book* (Nashville: Thomas Nelson, 2012), 47.

Chapter Six Is Heaven What I've Been Longing for All Along?

1. Jonathan Edwards, *Heaven, A World of Love* (Amityville, NY: Calvary Press, 1999), 28–29.

Chapter Seven Are There Rewards in Heaven?

1. "Wrong Miss Universe Winner Announced," YouTube, Associated Press, December 21, 2015, https://www.youtube.com/watch?v=eVs08g68lyU.

2. "The Culture of Corinth," Helpmewithbiblestudy.org, 2015, accessed September 22, 2023, http://helpmewithbiblestudy.org/16History/CityCorinth.aspx.

3. Amy Carmichael, *Gold Cord* (Fort Washington, PA: CLC Publications, 1982), 69–70.

Chapter Eight When Will There Be a New Heaven and a New Earth?

1. "The New Heaven and New Earth as Depicted in Revelation 21–22," BibleProject, December 24, 2017, https://bibleproject.com/articles/new-heaven-new -earth.

2. Anne Graham Lotz, *Heaven: My Father's House* (Nashville: Thomas Nelson, 2001), 49.

3. Randy Alcorn, "Heaven and the New Earth from the Bible and C. S. Lewis," C. S. Lewis Institute, January 2, 2022, https://www.cslewisinstitute.org/resources /heaven-and-the-new-earth-from-the-bible-and-c-s-lewis.

4. Alcorn, "Heaven and the New Earth."

5. Ted Mulder, "In 1952, Young Florence Chadwick Stepped into the Waters of the Pacific Ocean," Sermon Central, accessed October 4, 2023, https://www .sermoncentral.com/sermon-illustrations/31983/1n-1952-young-florence-chadwick -stepped-into-by-ted-mulder.

Chapter Nine How Does Heaven Change the Way We Live Today?

1. *Robin Hood*, directed by Ridley Scott (Universal City, CA: Universal Pictures, 2010). See movie clip at https://www.youtube.com/watch?v=H07DuZQ-rLQ.

2. Albert Barnes, *Barnes' Notes on the Old and New Testaments: Revelation* (Grand Rapids: Baker, 1996), 454.

3. Mark Hitchcock, *55 Answers to Questions about Life after Death* (Portland: Multnomah, 2005), 175.

4. David Jeremiah, *Revealing the Mysteries of Heaven* (Southlake, TX: Breakfast for Seven, 2020), 250–51.

5. Victor Hugo, quoted in Stuart Strachan Jr., "That Future Life," The Pastor's Workshop, October 8, 2020, https://thepastorsworkshop.com/that-future-life.

ABOUT
THE AUTHOR

Originally from Scotland, **Sheila Walsh** is an author, Bible teacher, and television host. She has spoken around the world to over six million people and now hosts numerous shows on TBN, America's most-watched faith and family channel, including the flagship show, *Praise*, and the talk show *Better Together*, reaching a potential daily audience of two billion people through TV and the TBN app.

A two-time Grammy-nominated recording artist, Sheila has recorded over twenty-five albums.

She loves making the Bible practical and sharing how God met her at her lowest point and helped her to rise up again.

Sheila's books have sold almost six million copies and include multiple bestsellers: *It's Okay Not to Be Okay*, *Praying Women*, and *Holding On When You Want to Let Go*.

She and her husband, Barry, live in Texas with their crazy little dog, Maggie. Their son, Christian, is a clinical psychologist.

Connect with Sheila:

SheilaWalsh.com

 @SheilaWalshConnects

 @SheilaWalsh1

 @SheilaWalsh

Watch Sheila on the Trinity Broadcasting Network, America's largest faith and family network.